T0253911

Microsoft Azure Cosmos DB Revealed

A Multi-Modal Database
Designed for the Cloud

José Rolando Guay Paz

Apress®

Microsoft Azure Cosmos DB Revealed

José Rolando Guay Paz
Beach Park, Illinois, USA

ISBN-13 (pbk): 978-1-4842-3350-4   ISBN-13 (electronic): 978-1-4842-3351-1
https://doi.org/10.1007/978-1-4842-3351-1

Library of Congress Control Number: 2018930529

Copyright © 2018 by José Rolando Guay Paz

This work is subject to copyright. All rights are reserved by the Publisher, whether the whole or part of the material is concerned, specifically the rights of translation, reprinting, reuse of illustrations, recitation, broadcasting, reproduction on microfilms or in any other physical way, and transmission or information storage and retrieval, electronic adaptation, computer software, or by similar or dissimilar methodology now known or hereafter developed.

Trademarked names, logos, and images may appear in this book. Rather than use a trademark symbol with every occurrence of a trademarked name, logo, or image we use the names, logos, and images only in an editorial fashion and to the benefit of the trademark owner, with no intention of infringement of the trademark.

The use in this publication of trade names, trademarks, service marks, and similar terms, even if they are not identified as such, is not to be taken as an expression of opinion as to whether or not they are subject to proprietary rights.

While the advice and information in this book are believed to be true and accurate at the date of publication, neither the authors nor the editors nor the publisher can accept any legal responsibility for any errors or omissions that may be made. The publisher makes no warranty, express or implied, with respect to the material contained herein.

Cover image designed by Freepik

Managing Director: Welmoed Spahr
Editorial Director: Todd Green
Acquisitions Editor: Jonathan Gennick
Development Editor: Laura Berendson
Technical Reviewer: Warner Chaves
Coordinating Editor: Jill Balzano
Copy Editor: Mary Behr
Compositor: SPi Global
Indexer: SPi Global
Artist: SPi Global

Distributed to the book trade worldwide by Springer Science+Business Media New York, 233 Spring Street, 6th Floor, New York, NY 10013. Phone 1-800-SPRINGER, fax (201) 348-4505, e-mail orders-ny@springer-sbm.com, or visit www.springeronline.com. Apress Media, LLC is a California LLC and the sole member (owner) is Springer Science + Business Media Finance Inc (SSBM Finance Inc). SSBM Finance Inc is a **Delaware** corporation.

For information on translations, please e-mail rights@apress.com, or visit www.apress.com/ rights-permissions.

Apress titles may be purchased in bulk for academic, corporate, or promotional use. eBook versions and licenses are also available for most titles. For more information, reference our Print and eBook Bulk Sales web page at www.apress.com/bulk-sales.

Any source code or other supplementary material referenced by the author in this book is available to readers on GitHub via the book's product page, located at www.apress.com/9781484233504. For more detailed information, please visit www.apress.com/source-code.

Printed on acid-free paper

To the Lord, Jesus Christ

*To my wife, Karina, and my daughters,
Sara and Samantha*

Table of Contents

About the Author

José Rolando Guay Paz is a professional developer with more than
20 years of experience in implementing database-backed applications. He
was among the first in Central America to build commercial applications
using Microsoft .NET. He has deep experience in Oracle Database and
SQL Server, and he is an MCPD in ASP.NET 3.5/4.0, an MCSD in web
applications, and an MCTS in SQL Server 2012/2014. José's native
language is Spanish, he is fluent in English, and he has learned some
French. He holds a bachelor's degree in Computer Science and a master's
degree in Finance.

About the Technical Reviewer

Warner Chaves is a SQL Server MCM, Data Platform MVP, and Principal Consultant at Pythian, a Canada-based global company specializing in database services and analytics. A brief stint in .NET programming led to his early DBA formation working for enterprise customers in Hewlett-Packard's ITO organization. From there he transitioned to his current position at Pythian, building and managing data solutions in many industry verticals while leading a highly talented team of data platform consultants.

Acknowledgments

I can't thank Jonathan Gennick enough for helping to make this book a reality, providing valuable advice, and pushing when needed. Thanks also go to Jill Balzano for keeping all things organized. The technical reviewer, Warner Chaves, was a key player in ensuring the quality of the content. And thank you to the many people at Apress who were involved in one way or another in this project.

CHAPTER 1

Introduction to Azure Cosmos DB

The database space has been greatly dominated by relational database management systems (or RDBMSs) such as Microsoft® SQL Server or Oracle. This dominance was made possible in part by the wide range of solutions that can be built on top of those systems but also because of the powerful products that are available. There is, however, a different approach to data management, commonly known as NoSQL. The term *NoSQL* stands for "non SQL" or "not only SQL" since SQL (Structured Query Language) is almost exclusively tied to relational systems. NoSQL databases have existed since the 1960s but it wasn't until the early 2000s that they gained a lot of popularity with companies like Facebook and Amazon implementing them and products such as MongoDB, Cassandra, and Redis becoming the choices for many developers.

In this chapter, I will introduce Azure Cosmos DB, Microsoft's NoSQL database, which is available in Microsoft Azure as a globally distributed, multi-node database service. We will examine what it is and its main features, but most importantly, at the end of the chapter, you will have a complete development environment that you can use for your applications.

© José Rolando Guay Paz 2018
J. R. Guay Paz, *Microsoft Azure Cosmos DB Revealed*,
https://doi.org/10.1007/978-1-4842-3351-1_1

What Is Azure Cosmos DB?

Azure Cosmos DB started in 2010 as an internal Microsoft project known as "Project Florence." The objective of the project was to address some of the problems that the Microsoft developers were facing with large Internet-scale applications. In 2015, the project was made available to external developers in Microsoft Azure and a new product was born under the name of DocumentDB. Finally, at the Microsoft Build 2017 conference, Azure Cosmos DB was officially launched with existing DocumentDB capabilities such as global distribution and horizontal scale with low latency and high throughput.

What's new in Azure Cosmos DB is that it natively supports multiple data models: key-value, documents, graph, columnar, and more that are currently being developed. This gives you the freedom to work with your data in the form that best describes it. It also supports multiple APIs for accessing data including DocumentDB SQL, MongoDB, Apache Cassandra, Graph, and Table.

Major Features

The following are some of the most important features of Azure Cosmos DB. There are many features in the product, but what follows are the ones that drove the implementation. They are what the product developers most had in mind. Most of these features were present since DocumentDB; however, with the evolution of the product, new features were introduced, making Azure Cosmos DB what is now. Many more features are under development.

Turnkey Global Distribution

Global distribution means that your databases can be distributed across different regions of Microsoft Azure and can be stored and accessible closer to your clients. This powerful functionality has a high degree of automation and performance. There is no need to handle complex configurations, replication downtime, high latency, or security concerns. Using the Microsoft Azure portal, all you need to do is select the regions where the database will be distributed and the portal will do the rest.

Multiple Data Models and APIs

With Azure Cosmos DB, you can select the data model that best represents your data. There is no need to think in terms of a rigid structure for the data. If, for example, you want to store user settings, you can use the key-value data model; if you want to work with orders, products, and payments, you can use a document data model. If your data is best described as relations between entities, then use a graph data model.

The DocumentDB API provides familiar SQL query capabilities. If you have an application built on MongoDB, you can use the MongoDB API transparently; in many cases there is no need to rewrite the application, only change the connection string. For key-value databases, you can use the Table API, which provides the same functionality as Azure Table storage but with the benefits of the Azure Cosmos DB engine. With the Graph API, you can use the Apache TinkerPop graph traversal language, Gremlin, or any other TinkerPop-compatible graph system like Apache Spark GraphX.

Elastically Scale Throughput and Storage on Demand

Throughput in Azure Cosmos DB can be configured in requests per second based on the requirements of your application. You can also change this configuration at any time.

You can use all the storage you need. There are no caps as to how much data you can store. Also, scaling databases is transparent and happens automatically based on the configuration you set for your account.

3

High Availability and Response Time

Azure Cosmos DB has a standing SLA of 99.99% availability and a latency in the 99th percentile regardless of the region. It also provides a guaranteed throughput and consistency.

Five Consistency Models

Azure Cosmos DB provides five different consistency models, from strong SQL-like consistency to NoSQL-like eventual consistency. It all depends on what your business or application needs.

Setting Up the Development Environment

To develop applications with Azure Cosmos DB, I recommend using Microsoft Visual Studio 2017. The main reason for this recommendation is that it is very easy to build, test, and deploy applications for Microsoft Azure. Another reason is that Visual Studio has a free edition called Visual Studio Community Edition that has all the capabilities we need to develop applications with Azure Cosmos DB.

Installing Microsoft Visual Studio

If you already have Visual Studio 2017 installed, you can skip this section. To obtain Visual Studio, all you need to do is the following:

1. Open your browser and go to www.visualstudio.com/. The page is shown in Figure 1-1.

2. From the *Download Visual Studio* drop-down, select *Community 2017*. If you have a license for a different edition, you can download it by selecting it from the options.

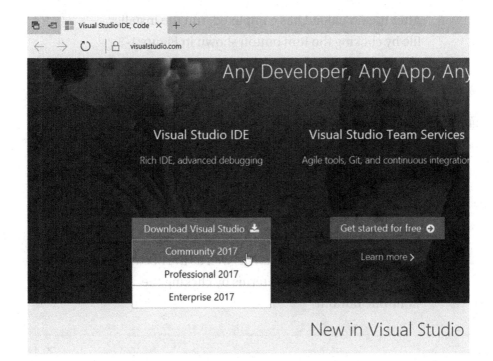

Figure 1-1. *Download Microsoft Visual Studio 2017*

3. After selecting an edition to download, you will be redirected to a new page where your download will start.

4. Save the installer file in a folder by clicking the Save button, as shown in Figure 1-2.

Figure 1-2. *Save the installer file to a folder*

5. After the download has completed, run the installer file by clicking the Run button shown in Figure 1-3.

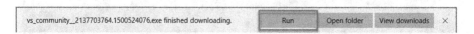

Figure 1-3. *Run the installer file*

6. You may be prompted to authorize the file to run. Select *Yes* in the prompt window.

7. The first window in the installation program (shown in Figure 1-4) will show you links to read the Microsoft Privacy Statement as well as the license terms. Accept the license terms by clicking the Continue button.

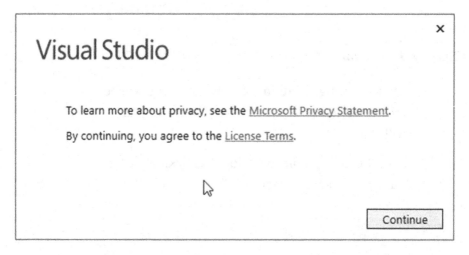

Figure 1-4. *Visual Studio license terms and privacy statement window*

8. Once you click the button, the installation program will download the most current list of options to install, as seen in Figure 1-5.

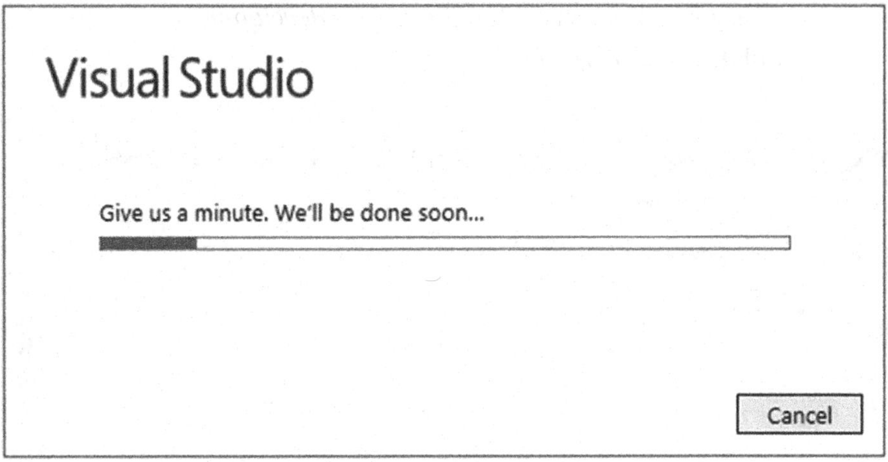

Figure 1-5. *Downloading installation options*

9.   After the options are downloaded, they will
     be displayed so you can select the necessary
     components for the types of applications you will
     develop. Figure 1-6 shows these components. In this
     case, you will select *ASP.NET and web development*
     and *Azure development*.

Figure 1-6. *Selecting Visual Studio components to install*

10.   Leave the default location to copy the files and click
      the Install button.

11. The program will start downloading the necessary files from Microsoft and install Visual Studio, as shown in Figure 1-7.

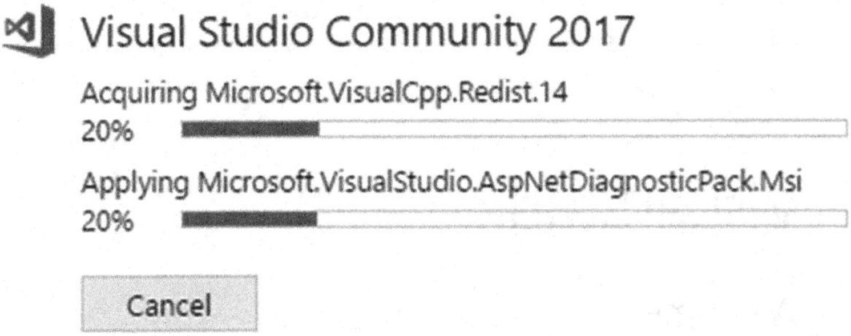

◁ Visual Studio Community 2017

Acquiring Microsoft.VisualCpp.Redist.14
20%

Applying Microsoft.VisualStudio.AspNetDiagnosticPack.Msi
20%

Cancel

Figure 1-7. *Downloading and installing Visual Studio Community 2017*

12. Once the installation has completed, you will need to restart your PC. Figure 1-8 shows the window requiring you to restart your PC. You can choose to do so later but it is not recommended to try to launch Visual Studio before restarting the PC.

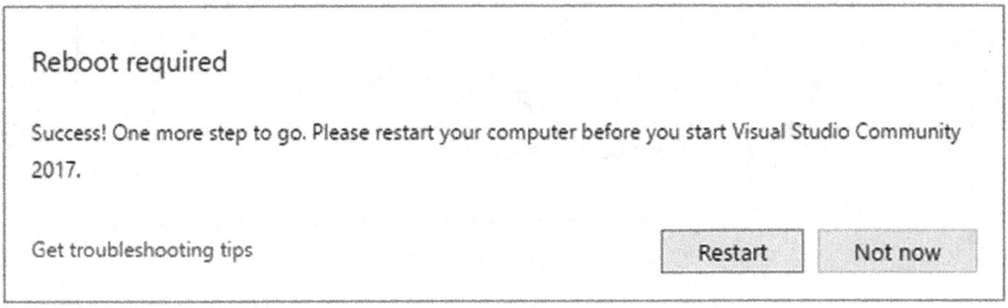

Reboot required

Success! One more step to go. Please restart your computer before you start Visual Studio Community 2017.

Get troubleshooting tips   Restart   Not now

Figure 1-8. *Restart your PC after installation has completed*

13. Figure 1-9 shows Visual Studio's welcome window.
     After you restart, you can launch Visual Studio. It
     will ask you to sign in with a Microsoft account such
     as an Outlook.com or Office 365 account.

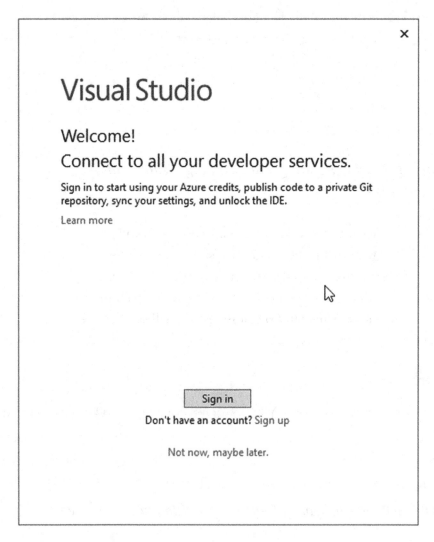

Figure 1-9. Sign in with a Microsoft account

14. Next, you will be asked to configure some settings
for Visual Studio, as shown in Figure 1-10. For the
development settings, select *Web Development*. For
the color theme, choose the color you like the most.

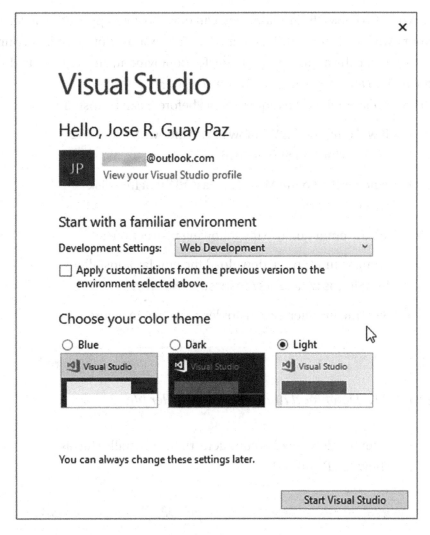

Figure 1-10. *Visual Studio's welcome window and environment settings*

15. That's it. You now have Visual Studio installed and
     running.

Installing the Azure Cosmos DB Emulator

With Azure Cosmos DB Emulator, you can develop your application locally
on your own computer without creating an Azure subscription or incurring
any costs. Once the application is ready for deployment, all you need to do
is to switch to an Azure Cosmos DB subscription.

The emulator has some requirements before it can be installed:

- It will only run on Windows 10, Windows Server 2012
  R2, or Windows Server 2016.

- It needs 2GB of RAM and at least 10GB of free disk
  space for storage.

To install the emulator, use the following instructions:

- Using your browser, download the emulator installer
  from `https://aka.ms/cosmosdb-emulator`.

- Save the installer file in a folder, as shown in Figure 1-11.

Figure 1-11. *Download and save the installer file*

- After the download is complete, run the installer file as
  shown in Figure 1-12.

Figure 1-12. *Run the installer file*

- Figure 1-13 shows the first window in the installation
  program. Check the box to accept the license agreement
  and click the Install button.

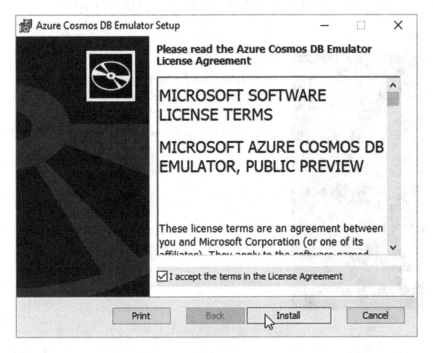

Figure 1-13. *Accept the license agreement and click the Install button*

- You may be prompted to authorize the file to run.
  Select *Yes* in the prompt window.

- The installation will happen very quickly and then the final window will give you the option to launch the emulator. Check the box to launch the emulator and then click the Finish button, as shown in Figure 1-14.

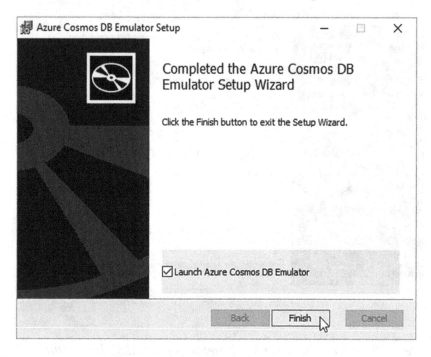

Figure 1-14. *Installation of the Azure Cosmos DB Emulator is complete*

- After you click the Finish button, the emulator starts and launches the web interface (shown in Figure 1-15). This will indicate that the installation was successful.

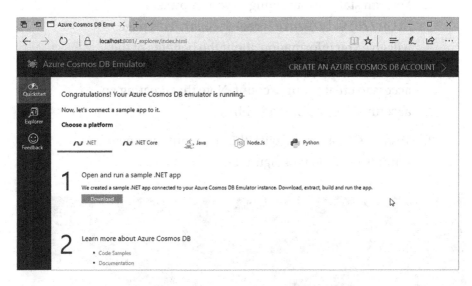

Figure 1-15. *Azure Cosmos DB Emulator web interface*

With these tools, you have now set up a development environment to create applications that use Azure Cosmos DB.

Creating a Microsoft Azure Account and Subscription

Microsoft has made the process of creating an Azure account very easy. The account will give you access to Azure, but in order to use the products you must also create a subscription. The subscription you will create now is based on the free tier, which gives you (at the time of this writing) one month and $200 in credits to use. To create your account, perform the following steps:

1. You can start by navigating in your browser to http://bit.ly/azure-free-account. This page will give you information about the benefits of the free tier in Microsoft Azure and will also give you access to create your account. Note that creating an account does not cost anything.

2. To create an account, click the green button labeled "Start free," shown in Figure 1-16.

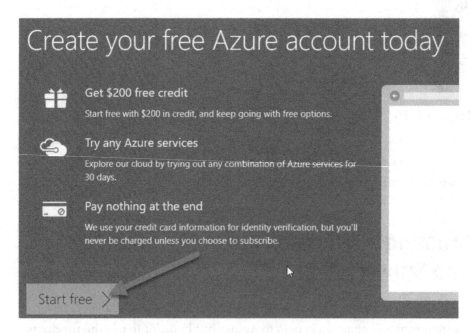

Figure 1-16. *Click the "Start free" button to start creating your Azure account*

3. On the following page, you need to sign up with
    your Microsoft account. If you don't have one, you
    can create one by following the link *Create a new
    Microsoft account* at the bottom of the page, as
    shown in Figure 1-17.

Figure 1-17. *Sign in with your Microsoft account*

4. Once you have signed in or created a new Microsoft
    account, your Azure account is active.

5. Now it is time to create your subscription. For the
    subscription, you will be presented with a four-step
    form. At the end of the four steps you will have an
    active subscription based on the free tier. The first step
    is information about you, as shown in Figure 1-18.

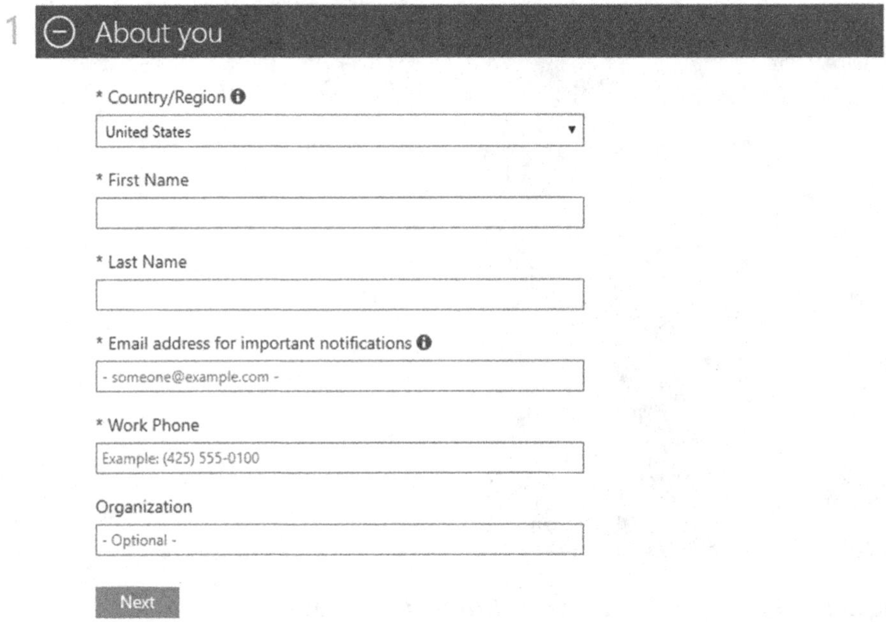

1 ⊖ About you

* Country/Region ❶

United States   ▼

* First Name

* Last Name

* Email address for important notifications ❶

- someone@example.com -

* Work Phone

Example: (425) 555-0100

Organization

- Optional -

Next

Figure 1-18. *Information about you to create your Azure account
and subscription*

6. The second step is to add a valid mobile phone
    number to validate your identity. It should be a
    standard mobile number; VOIP numbers are not
    accepted. The step is shown in Figure 1-19. This is
    the first identity verification. There will be a second
    one following this step. Once you enter your mobile
    phone number, click the "Send text message" button
    to get a verification code. Once you receive that code,
    type it into the third box and click the "Verify code"
    button.

Figure 1-19. *Enter your mobile phone number to validate your*
identity

7. In step three, the process will ask for a credit card.
    You will need to enter the credit card information
    along with the billing address associated with the
    card. The information is shown in Figure 1-20. At
    this point, *the credit card information is just for
    identity verification and will not be charged until you
    switch to a paid type subscription.*

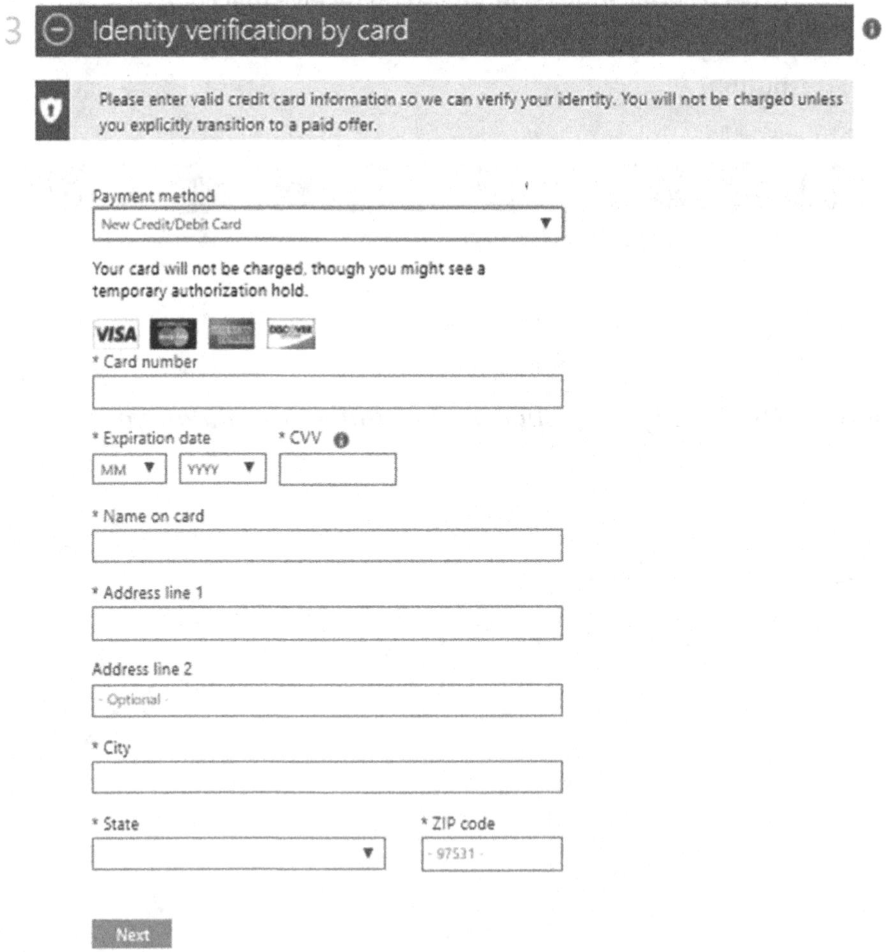

Figure 1-20. *Enter the credit card information to be used in your subscription*

8. The final step in the subscription process is to accept the subscription agreement, offer details, and privacy statement shown in Figure 1-21. Just check the box to agree and click the "Sign up" button. You will be redirected to the Azure portal.

Figure 1-21. *Accept the agreement, offer details, and privacy statement*

Provisioning an Azure Cosmos DB Database

Now that you have created your account and subscription, you are ready to provision your first Azure Cosmos DB database. The process is very simple. Just follow the next steps, which are illustrated in Figure 1-22.

1. From the Azure portal, click in the big plus sign in the top left corner. This will open the services categories panel where you can select the new service to be added.

2. From the categories panel, select *Databases*. This will open the services under the Databases category.

3. Select *Azure Cosmos DB*. The Azure Cosmos DB account form panel is opened.

4. You now need to fill the Azure Cosmos DB account form.

a. ID: This field identifies the Azure Cosmos DB account. Enter a name that uniquely identifies your account. A green checkmark at the end of the field will show up if the name is valid.

b. API: For this field, you need to select between Gremlin (graph), MongoDB, SQL (DocumentDB), or Table (key-value).

c. Subscription: Select the new free subscription you just created in the previous section.

d. Resource Group: A resource group is a collection of resources or services in Microsoft Azure that share the same lifecycle, permissions, and policies. Create a new resource group by entering its name or select one from the list if you have created one. Since this is the first resource being created, you will need to enter the resource group name and select "Create new."

e. Location: This field refers to the Azure region where the database will be first created. Select the one closest to you, or if you know your target market, the one closest to it to get better network speed.

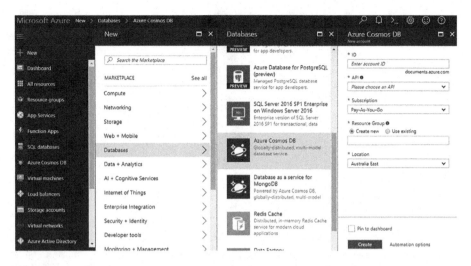

Figure 1-22. *Creating a new Azure Cosmos DB database*

Summary

In this chapter, I introduced you to Azure Cosmos DB and its major features. You read about global distribution and how it helps get the data closer to your application's users and how it allows you to have a higher availability, which is also guaranteed in the standard SLA. I explained the different data models and supported APIs and also briefly mentioned scalability and consistency.

You now have a complete development environment with Microsoft Visual Studio 2017 and the Azure Cosmos DB Emulator. These are the tools to develop, test, and deploy your applications to Azure. Finally, you have created your Microsoft Azure account and subscription, and you have provisioned your first Azure Cosmos DB database.

In the next chapter, we will examine these concepts in detail.

CHAPTER 2

Learning Azure Cosmos DB Concepts

To properly implement and use an Azure Cosmos DB database, it is very important to understand several key concepts about the internals of the service. In this chapter, I am going to examine concepts such as global distribution, partitioning, and consistency to provide a solid foundation upon which you will be able to build robust, scalable, and secure applications.

Understanding these concepts is the best way to leverage all of the potential and capabilities of Azure Cosmos DB. It's important that you know what you can do and that you understand why things work in a certain way.

Understanding Global Distribution

Microsoft Azure is available globally in over 30 regions, and it is constantly growing. Azure Cosmos DB is available in all of the existing regions, but because it is internally classified as a *Ring 0 Azure Service*, it will be available in any new region by default. Azure Cosmos DB databases can be distributed across these regions to provide higher availability, scalability, and throughput (I will discuss throughput later in this chapter).

© José Rolando Guay Paz 2018
J. R. Guay Paz, *Microsoft Azure Cosmos DB Revealed*,
https://doi.org/10.1007/978-1-4842-3351-1_2

Global distribution is a comparable concept to what replication is for relational databases; the difference is that everything is handled by Azure and you don't need complex configurations either at the database level or the application level.

To understand how simple the process to distribute a database is, see Figure 2-1. It shows the database created in Chapter 1 in the Azure portal. I have clicked the *Replicate data globally* option on the left menu and it displays a world map with all the available Azure regions.

For this database, the region where the database was created is shown in a solid light blue hexagon with a white checkmark. The available regions are shown in hexagons with a white background and a solid dark blue border. The regions where the database will be distributed (or replicated) are shown in hexagons with a solid dark blue background with a white checkmark.

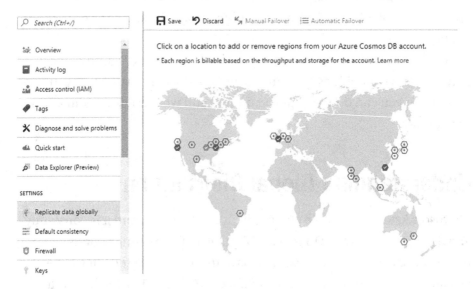

Figure 2-1. *Azure Cosmos DB database distributed to four regions*

Introducing Write and Read Regions

When the database was first created, it was based on only one region. This default configuration defines the first (and only) region where a database accepts read and write operations. When you distribute the database to more regions, the new regions automatically become read regions.

When this new configuration is in place, you also enable the failover feature. By default, failover happens manually, meaning you will have to log into the Azure portal and switch reads to a different region if the designated read region is not available.

Failover can also happen automatically. With automatic failover, each region has a priority in the list of read regions. If for any reason the designated read region is not available, Azure will switch to the next available read region based on the defined priorities. In Figure 2-2, you can see how the database has one write region and two read regions with automatic failover. Each of the read regions has a priority, and applications will read from the region at the top of the list. Azure will determine whenever the region becomes unavailable and will then choose the next region in the list.

You cannot configure the database to have more than one write region. This feature is not available at this point. A configuration known as *multi-master* can be implemented but it requires two databases and is the closest to having more than one write region. Normally, you would want to implement a multi-master configuration to allow writes to regions where users creating content are closer, providing even lower latency.

When having multiple write and/or read regions there is an associated concept that needs to be learned. This is the concept of *consistency*. You will learn about consistency next.

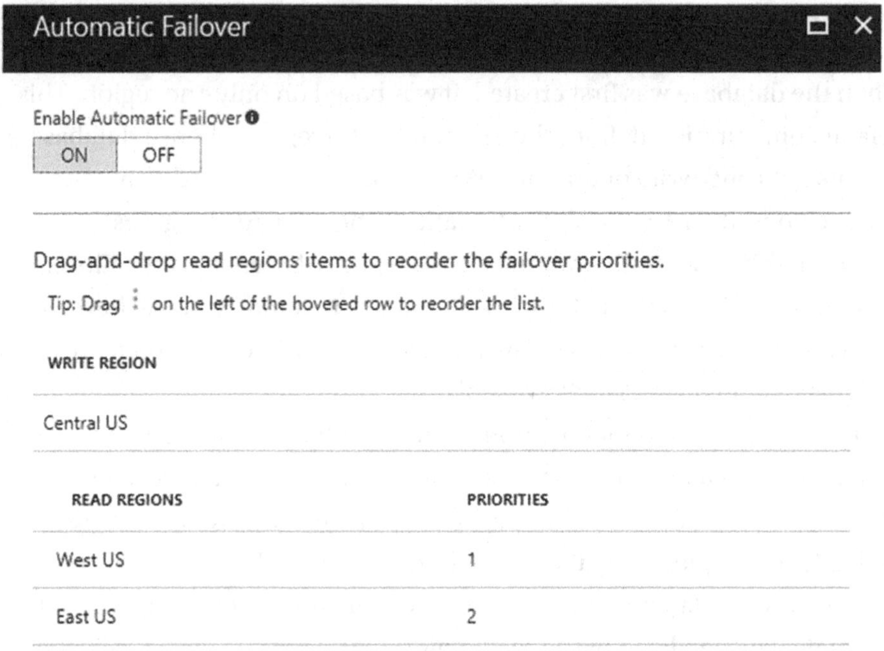

Automatic Failover	□ ✕

Enable Automatic Failover ❶

| ON | OFF |

Drag-and-drop read regions items to reorder the failover priorities.

Tip: Drag ⠿ on the left of the hovered row to reorder the list.

WRITE REGION

Central US

READ REGIONS	PRIORITIES
West US	1
East US	2

Figure 2-2. *Azure Cosmos DB database with automatic failover and two read regions*

Understanding the Consistency Models

Consistency defines the rules under which distributed data is available to users. What this means is that when new data is available (i.e. new or updated data) in a distributed database, the consistency model determines when the data is available to users for reads.

Despite having defined and proposed over 50 different consistency models for distributed databases throughout history, the most significant (and commercially available) are *strong* and *eventual*. The problem here is that there is no real consensus about widely used scenarios that can create enough interest for database products to implement them. Most of the proposed consistency models try to solve only a very specific problem or scenario.

Azure Cosmos DB implements five different consistency models. Besides *strong* and *eventual,* there are three additional consistency models. These are the *bounded staleness, session*, and *consistent prefix*. With these five models, you will be able to determine the most appropriate model for your application based on availability and latency.

These additional consistency models are based on the work of the scientist and Turing Award (`https://en.wikipedia.org/wiki/Turing_Award`) winner Leslie Lamport, PhD (`www.lamport.org/`).

When deciding which consistency model to use, you need to understand that they are all bound to elements such as throughput and latency. As you will see when examining each of the five consistency models, on one end is *strong consistency*, which will provide highest latency of all, guaranteeing consistent reads across the entire read regions. On the other end, *eventual consistency* will provide the lowest latency at a cost of a high probability of not showing the latest data when reading from different regions. The other three consistency models provide values in-between these extremes for latency and throughput. It will depend on what your application needs. Happily, you have several options.

Scope of Consistency

The granularity of consistency is scoped to a single user request. A write request may correspond to an insert, replace, update, or delete transaction. As with writes, a read/query transaction is also scoped to a single user request. The user may be required to paginate over a large result-set, spanning multiple partitions, but each read transaction is scoped to a single page and served from within a single partition. I will discuss partitions later in this chapter.

Strong Consistency Model

An Azure Cosmos DB account with a strong consistency model guarantees that any read of an item (such as a customer record) will return the most recent version of such item. This is important because it is the same consistency model typically implemented in relational database systems. Because we are working in a distributed environment, strong consistency guarantees that a write operation is visible only after the majority of the replicas have been committed durably with the write. A client will never see a partially committed or incomplete write.

In Figure 2-3 you can see how a strong consistency model is implemented in an Azure Cosmos DB account.

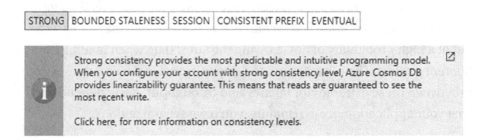

Figure 2-3. *Azure Cosmos DB account with strong consistency model*

When strong consistency is configured for the Azure Cosmos DB account, reads are only as fast as the latency among all regions involved in the write. Because of this, an account with strong consistency can only be associated to one Azure region. You use strong consistency when writes are important and need to be fast, and applications don't need to read the data instantly. See in Figure 2-4 how the Azure portal blocks the ability to distribute the account to multiple regions when using strong consistency.

The current Default Consistency of your account does not allow data to be replicated globally.

To allow global replication, change the Default Consistency to Bounded Staleness (with a Maximum Lag of at least 100,000 operations and at least 5 minutes), Session, Consistent Prefix, or Eventual consistency.

To change the Default Consistency, go to "Settings > Default Consistency"

Figure 2-4. *Strong consistency prevents the Azure Cosmos DB from being distributed to multiple regions*

At the same time, if an account was defined with a different consistency model, such as session, the Azure portal will not allow you to change the consistency model to strong. In fact, it won't even give you the option, as shown in Figure 2-5.

| BOUNDED STALENESS | SESSION | CONSISTENT PREFIX | EVENTUAL |

Session consistency is most widely used consistency level both for single region as well as, globally distributed applications.

It provides write latencies, availability and read throughput comparable to that of eventual consistency but also provides the consistency guarantees that suit the needs of applications written to operate in the context of a user.

Click here, for more information on consistency levels.

Figure 2-5. *Strong consistency is not available once an Azure Cosmos DB account is distributed to multiple regions*

Eventual Consistency Model

When using the eventual consistency model, it is guaranteed that all of the replicas will eventually converge to reflect the most recent write. In terms of data consistency, this is a very weak model because users may read values that are older than those defined by the most recent write; however, it does offer the lowest latency of all consistency models for both reads and writes. Low latency is achieved by not requiring every single replica (region) to read the same value after each write. Data replication happens in the background and will be complete at some point; it is just that application reads are not stopped until all of the regions are synchronized.

Eventual consistency is used in many NoSQL and relational database systems. It is useful in scenarios where reads need to happen as soon as possible even if they don't display the most recent version of the data. It is only guaranteed that all replicas will be consistent at some point; you just don't know exactly when that will be.

Bounded Staleness Consistency Model

With bounded staleness, reads may lag behind writes by at most K operations or a t time interval. For an account with only one region, K must be between 10 and 1,000,000 operations, and between 100,000 and 1,000,000 operations if the account is globally distributed. For t, the permitted time intervals are between 5 seconds and 1 day for accounts in one region, and between 5 minutes and 1 day for globally distributed accounts.

For example, if an account is in only one region and configured with a lag of 10 operations and 5 seconds, then if the latest write was more than 5 seconds ago or more than 10 operations ago, it is guaranteed that the user will see the most recent version of the data.

This consistency model is suitable for applications that need writes with strong consistency and low latency, and reads that are consistent after a predictable number of operations or time interval. In addition, the monotonic read guarantees exist within a region both inside and outside the staleness window.

An Azure Cosmos DB account can be globally distributed to any number of Azure regions when using bounded staleness consistency. In Figure 2-6, you can see the configuration options to enable the bounded staleness consistency model.

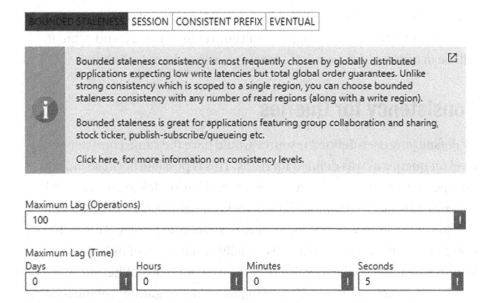

Figure 2-6. *Configuration of a bounded staleness consistency model*

Session Consistency Model

The session consistency model is named so because the consistency level is scoped at the client session. What this means is that any reads or writes are always current within the same session and they are monotonic. During the life of a session, any write is immediately available for read and will be available for other sessions as soon as the data is replicated to the rest of the regions.

This model provides high read throughput and low latency writes and reads. This is the default consistency model for any new Azure Cosmos DB account and you can distribute it to any number of Azure regions.

Consistent Prefix Consistency Model

The last consistency model is consistent prefix. This model is similar to the eventual consistency model; however, it guarantees that reads never see out-of-order writes. For example, if your application writes 1, then 2, and

33

finally 3, users will see 1, or 1 and 2, or 1 and 2 and 3, but will never see 1 and 3. Eventually, all Azure regions will converge to 1 and 2 and 3, but it will be in order, which translates into higher speeds and reliability.

Consistency for Queries

By default, any user-defined resource would have the same consistency level for queries as was defined for reads. This is possible because indexes are updated synchronously on any insert, replace, or delete on any item in an Azure Cosmos DB container (I'll discuss containers later in this chapter).

You can also change the index update strategy to be lazy. This will boost the performance of writes, especially in scenarios of bulk data import where the application is primarily used for reads. What you need to be aware of is that, when changing to lazy, regardless of the read consistency level, queries will have a consistency level of eventual.

The consistency level of a specific query can be adjusted on every request using the API.

Understanding Partitioning

Partitioning is a key concept for Azure Cosmos DB. It is what enables millisecond response time at any scale. A good partitioning scheme is crucial to your application because it directly affects its performance.

What Are Containers?

Azure Cosmos DB provides three types of containers for your data: **collections** (for documents), **tables,** and **graphs**. Containers are logical resources that group together one or more physical partitions. Partitions are determined by a partition key in a container. Each partition has a fixed amount of SSD-backed storage associated with it and it is locally replicated for high availability. Containers don't have any restrictions in terms of amount of storage or throughput; they can grow as large as needed and will scale as well.

Figure 2-7 shows how containers and partitions are defined. Note that regardless of the type of container, they all work the same. This is important in terms of predictability of performance because it guarantees the same response time independent of the type of data you are working with.

Partition management is transparent and managed entirely by Azure Cosmos DB. There is no need for custom code for this purpose, nor is any additional configuration required for the account or container other than defining the partition key.

Collections can have a fixed storage limit (up to 10GB) or can be unlimited. The configuration will be determined by the necessary throughput for the application.

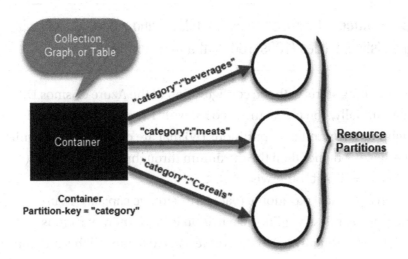

Figure 2-7. *Containers and partitions*

How Does Partitioning Work?

You need to define a partition key and a row key for each item in your container. These key combinations uniquely identify the item. The partition key determines the logical partition for your data and informs Azure Cosmos DB of the boundary for distributing such data across different partitions.

Azure Cosmos DB uses hash-based partitioning. When you write an item, Azure Cosmos DB hashes the partition key value and uses that to determine which partition it should store the item in. All items with the same partition key are stored in the same physical partition. Given this characteristic, **choosing the right partition key is crucial and should be done based on a key that provides a wide range of values and has even access patterns**.

Best Practice   Microsoft recommends having a partition key with many distinct values (100s-1000s at a minimum).

Partitioning starts with the configuration of the Azure Cosmos DB account. Initially, you create the account with T requests per second throughput. The number of partitions (N) that are created are determined by whether T is higher than the maximum throughput per partition (t). If so, then $N = T / t$, otherwise $N = 1$.

When a physical partition p reaches its storage capacity, Azure Cosmos DB seamlessly splits the partition into two new partitions $p1$ and $p2$, with roughly half of the values on each one. All this is managed transparently to your application.

If your provisioned throughput is higher than $t * N$, then Azure Cosmos DB splits the necessary partitions to support the required throughput.

Designing for Partitioning

I have mentioned the importance of choosing the right partition key for your application. There are two key considerations when choosing the partition key.

Boundary for Query and Transactions

Transactions in Azure Cosmos DB provide ACID guarantees; however, a particular consideration is that each transaction happens within the boundaries of a single partition. If your partition key does not generate a good number of partitions, then you will have problems scaling your application. On the other hand, if it creates too many of them (e.g. one document on each partition) you may end up with problems with cross-partition transactions in triggers and stored procedures.

Your partition key should balance the requirements for transactions versus the requirements for distributing the entities across partitions to scale the solution. Ideally, your partition key will enable you to efficiently query the data and will have enough cardinality to ensure your application can scale properly.

No Storage and Performance Bottlenecks

The partition key should allow for writes to be distributed as evenly as possible across different values. Requests to the same partition key cannot exceed the throughput for a single partition and are throttled. It is therefore necessary that the partition key will not result in partitions that are always requested and/or partitions that allocate most of the data. If this is the case, then a different partition key should be considered.

Understanding Throughput

Azure Cosmos DB supports completely different data models (documents, tables, and graphs) so establishing a consistent model to handle requests was paramount. To solve this problem, Microsoft introduced a normalized quantity called *request unit* based on the computational requirements to serve a request. Using request units, it is much easier to establish a consistent method for billing requests across the different data models. The number of requests units per operation is deterministic and can be obtained on every request by reading the response headers.

I have mentioned that Azure Cosmos DB has predictable performance, and this is achieved by provisioning a specific amount of request units (RU) per second, and this amount is what is called *throughput*. **Throughput is reserved in units of 100s of requests units per second**. You can think of request units as the currency of throughput because they are used to determine your bill.

An application's load changes over time and using the Azure portal you can increase or decrease the reserved throughput to fit your application's needs. There is no impact to the availability of the collection when you change the throughput configuration, and the new configuration normally goes into effect within seconds.

Important   Azure Cosmos DB operates under a reservation model on throughput. This means that you will be billed by how much reserved throughput you have as opposed to how much you actually use.

Specifying Request Unit Capacity

When defining a new collection, you need to configure the specific number of request units per second you want reserved for the container. Based on this number, Azure Cosmos DB allocates physical partitions to host the collection and it will manage the data across partitions as it grows.

If the collection has a fixed storage capacity, the reserved throughput can be between 400 and 10,000 request units per second. If it has unlimited capacity, the throughput can be between 2,500 and 100,000 requests units per second.

Estimating Throughput

A request unit represents the processing needed to read a single 1KB item with 10 property values (excluding system properties). A request to create, replace, or delete the same item will need more processing power and therefore more request units.

There is no better way to estimate throughput than by using the request unit calculator (`http://bit.ly/cosmos-db-ru-calc`) shown in Figure 2-8. The calculator can estimate the request units as well as the approximate storage need based on the information provided.

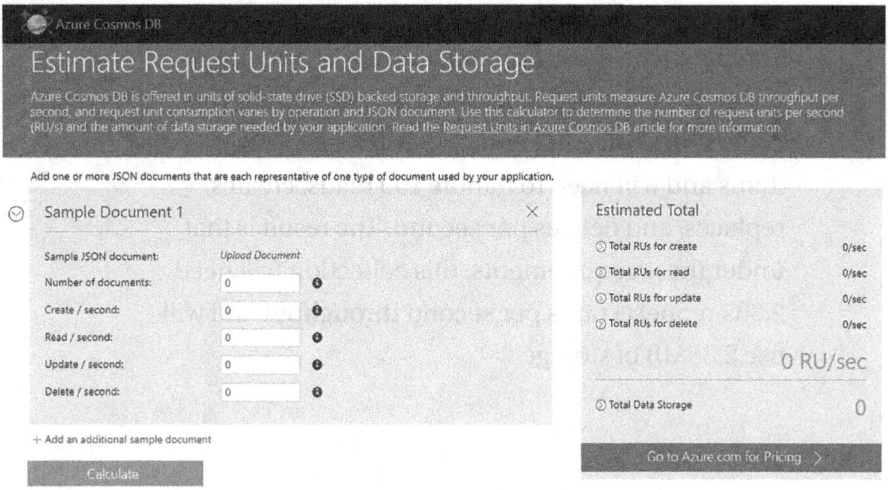

Figure 2-8. *Request unit calculator*

To use it, you need to do the following steps:

1. Upload a sample JSON file that represents an item in your collection, such as `sample_file.json`.

```
{
    "id":"1",
    "firstname":"Jose",
    "lastname":"Guay"
}
```

2. You will need a second JSON file that represents the same item but with modified values to simulate a replace, such as `sample_file_modified.json`.

```
{
    "id":"1",
    "firstname":"Rolando",
    "lastname":"Guay"
}
```

3. You then type the estimated number of operations per second and number of items to be stored. The collection shown in Figure 2-9 will store 50,000 items and will need to handle 100 reads, creates, replaces, and deletes per second. The result is that under these requirements, this collection will need 2,385 requests units per second throughput and will use 2.35MB of storage.

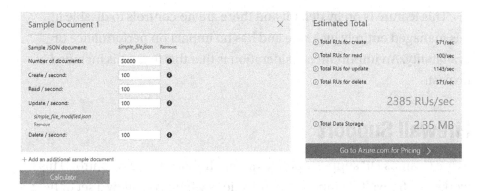

Figure 2-9. *Using the request unit calculator*

Implementing Security

Security in Azure Cosmos DB is implemented at several levels. There is a security layer at the storage level with the implementation of a technology named *encryption at rest*. At the network level, there is a *firewall* to enable access only to specified IPs or IP ranges, and data is always encrypted during transit. At the data access level, there is a configuration with *keys* and *tokens* to authenticate users and provide access to data. Finally, for increased availability a *replication strategy* ensures that data is never lost.

Encryption at Rest

The term *encryption at rest* commonly refers to encrypting data on permanent storage such as solid-state drives (SSDs) or hard disk drives (HDDs). Azure Cosmos DB stores the primary databases on SSD disks. Media attachments, replicas, and backups are stored in Azure Blob storage, which uses HDDs. Encryption at rest is implemented at all levels so all databases, media attachments, and backups are encrypted.

This feature is on by default and there are no controls to disable it. It is managed entirely by Azure and has no impact on performance or availability. An important consideration is that this feature is included at no cost.

Firewall Support

Azure Cosmos DB supports policy-driven, IP-based access control. This works as a firewall for inbound connections where you allow a set of IP addresses (or IP ranges) to access your Cosmos DB account. By default, this feature is off, as shown in Figure 2-10, which means anyone can connect to the Cosmos DB account, but you can turn it on to limit the computers accessing the database.

Figure 2-10. *The Azure Cosmos DB Firewall IP access control is turned off by default*

A common scenario is a website that uses an Azure Cosmos DB database account. You don't need to have all-in access to the database, only the IP of the website and your own IP address or IP range.

After you enable IP access control, you are given the option to add individual IP addresses or IP ranges (CIDR), as shown in Figure 2-11. You also have the option to limit access to the Azure portal to those IP addresses, although this setting is for now an all-or-nothing configuration; it won't allow settings per IP.

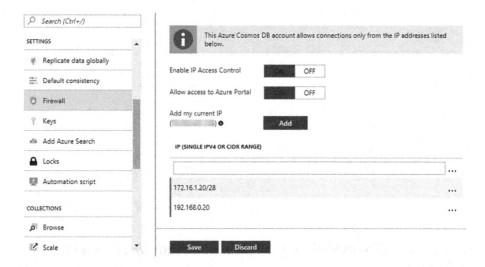

Figure 2-11. *Azure Cosmos DB Firewall with enabled IP access control*

After this configuration is saved, connections from IP addresses outside the defined set will be blocked by the firewall. According to the documentation from Microsoft (`http://bit.ly/cosmos-db-firewall`), if you enable IP access control, you will need to add specific IP addresses for the Azure portal to maintain access. Please see Figure 2-12 for the specific note.

If there are requests from IP addresses outside the allowed list, Azure Cosmos DB will return an HTTP response 404 Not Found with any details. This will ensure databases are kept hidden from unauthorized access.

☐ **Note**

When you enable an IP access control policy, you need to add the IP address for the Azure portal to maintain access. The portal IP addresses are:

Region	IP address
All regions except those specified below	104.42.195.92
Germany	51.4.229.218
China	139.217.8.252
US Gov Arizona	52.244.48.71

Figure 2-12. *Microsoft documentation note regarding access to Azure portal*

Securing Access to Data

With Azure Cosmos DB, you can use two different keys to authenticate users and provide access to data. They are *master keys* and *resource tokens*.

Master Keys

You use master keys to provide access to the administrative resources in the account, such as access to databases, users, and permissions. These keys are automatically created at the same time the account is created and can be regenerated at any time based on your security policy or if they have been compromised. Master keys can't be used to specify a more granular access to collections and documents.

Each Azure Cosmos DB account has two master keys: a primary master key and a secondary master key. Primary and secondary keys work exactly the same way and provide access to the same resources without any difference at all. The idea behind this implementation is that you can regenerate or rotate keys without interrupting access to the account or data.

Figure 2-13 shows the keys in an Azure Cosmos DB account. Note the two tabs for read-write and read-only keys. The information is the URI for accessing the database, the primary and secondary keys, and the primary and secondary connection strings. Next to each of the boxes is a button to copy to the clipboard the value in the box; the key boxes contain an extra button to regenerate them.

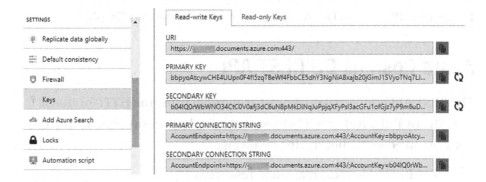

Figure 2-13.   *Read-write keys for an Azure Cosmos DB account*

Resource Tokens

Resource tokens provide access to resources within the database, such as partition keys, documents, attachments, and stored procedures; they are particularly useful when you want to provide access to a client that can't be trusted with a master key. They are created whenever a user is granted permissions to a specific resource and recreated when a permission account takes action by a POST, GET, or PULL request. Unlike keys, resource tokens cannot be managed in the Azure portal. They can only be managed using the Azure Cosmos DB API or client libraries.

A resource token has a validity period which by default is one hour. This validity period can be adjusted to up to five hours. It uses a hash token specifically designed for the resource, user, and permission.

Supported APIs

Azure Cosmos DB supports several APIs for resource and data management and several software development kits (SDKs) that encapsulate the functionality for them. At its core is the REST API, which provides a foundation for all actions that can be performed against an Azure Cosmos DB account. There are also other APIs such as DocumentDB, Mongo DB, Apache Cassandra, Table, and Graph.

Azure Cosmos DB REST API

The REST API interacts with Azure Cosmos DB using the HTTP protocol. As with any REST API, the HTTP verbs are used to inform what action to perform. In general, they are the following:

- POST: Used to create item resources

- GET: Used to read an item resource or a list of resources

- PUT: Used to replace an existing item resource

- DELETE: Used to delete an existing item resource

- HEAD: Used similarly to GET except it will only return the response headers

The destination URI for the API is based on the URI endpoint created for the database account. For example, if your database account was named ProductCatalog, then the base URI would be `https://productcatalog.documents.azure.com`.

Table 2-1 shows the base URIs for each of the resources in an Azure Cosmos DB account. There is a URI for each and every resource, and any action can be performed using the REST API.

To simplify the URIs in Table 2-1, please consider the following:

{base} = https://{databaseaccount}.documents.azure.com

I'll just use {base} instead so the URIs are shorter.

Table 2-1. *Base URIs for Each Resource in an Azure Cosmos DB Account (Source: http://bit.ly/cosmos-db-rest-uris)*

Resources	Base URI
Database	{base}/dbs/{db}
User	{base}/dbs/{db}/users/{user}
Permission	{base}/dbs/{db}/users/{user}/permissions/{perm}
Collection	{base}/dbs/{db}/colls/{coll}
Stored Procedure	{base}/dbs/{db}/colls/{coll}/sprocs/{sproc}
Trigger	{base}/dbs/{db}/colls/{coll}/triggers/{trigger}
UDF	{base}/dbs/{db}/colls/{coll}/udfs/{udf}
Document	{base}/dbs/{db}/colls/{coll}/docs/{doc}
Attachment	{base}/dbs/{db}/colls/{coll}/docs/{doc}/attachments/{attch}
Offer	{base}/offers/{offer}

Offers represent the collection's provisioned throughput. This throughput can be user-defined or predefined, and has an associated request unit (RU) rate limit which is reserved and available exclusively for the collection.

For example, to create a new database named Products in an account named ProductCatalog, you would use

```
POST https://productcatalog.documents.azure.com/dbs
{
    "id":"Products"
}
```

Note that you are using the verb *POST*, which instructs the API to create an item, in this case a database. The JSON information tells the API the id of the new database and the URI is composed using the account name. You can use a tool like Telerik Fiddler (`www.telerik.com/fiddler`) or Postman (`www.getpostman.com`) to test REST API calls.

The API then sends a response to the client that looks like this:

```
HTTP/1.1 201 Created
Content-Type: application/json
x-ms-request-charge: 4.95

...

{
    "id": "Products",
    "_rid": "UoBa5x==",
    "_self": "dbs/UoBa5x==/",
    "_ts": 1403525012,
    "_etag": "00000100-0000-0000-0000-f3a1366000e8",
    "_colls": "colls/",
    "_users": "users/"
}
```

In this particular case, the _rid property defines the encrypted value that internally identifies the new database, and it is the value that needs to be used for subsequent calls to, for example, create collections and read documents.

Note   It is important to understand that, depending on your preferred language and/or platform, you would (and should) be using an SDK specifically designed for it. It is far easier to interact with the SDK than to use the REST API directly. For more information about the Azure Cosmos DB REST API, visit `http://bit.ly/cosmos-db-rest-api`.

DocumentDB API

The DocumentDB API is built on top of the REST API and is implemented in several languages and platforms including .NET, Java, NodeJS, JavaScript, and Python via their respective SDKs.

Using the DocumentDB API you can query documents using a SQL syntax similar to the one used in Entity Framework, only extended to query JSON documents. You can also manage the account resources and perform actions such as create databases, collections, stored procedures, etc.

For example, in the previous section you created a new database using the REST API. Let's do the same now using the DocumentDB API in C#, as shown in Listing 2-1.

Listing 2-1. Creating a New Database Using DocumentDB API .NET SDK in C#

```
var dbUrl = "https://productcatalog.documents.azure.com/dbs";
var authKey = "the primary or secondary key for the account";
client = new DocumentClient(new Uri(dbUrl),authKey);
await client.CreateDatabaseAsync(new Database { Id = "Products" });
```

Note in Listing 2-1 that you still use the URLs for the endpoints as described in Table 2-1, and you are clearly using the master keys to access the resources. These two values are stored in variables that are later used to create a `DocumentClient` object. This object is used to interact with the Azure Cosmos DB account. Finally, the code calls the `CreateDatabaseAsync()` method, passing as a parameter an instance of a new `Database` object, and it is all done asynchronously.

The example in Listing 2-1 is very simple and it doesn't do much, but it is a good example of how to get started with the DocumentDB API SDK. The URLs and master key should be stored in a central location for easy and consistent access across the entire client application. The `AppSettings` section in the configuration file is a good candidate for such values.

Listing 2-3 shows a brief example of how to query the document shown in Listing 2-2. Note how the syntax for querying is very much the same as with SQL Server or Entity Framework.

Listing 2-2. Sample JSON Document

```
{
        "id": "Fruits",
        "products":[
                {"name":"Apple","price":0.50},
                {"name":"Banana","price":0.80},
                {"name":"Peach","price":0.60},
                {"name":"Grapes","price":1.00},
        ],
}
```

Listing 2-3. Querying the Sample JSON Document from Listing 2-2

```
SELECT p.name
FROM Products p
WHERE p.id = "Fruits"
AND p.products.price > 0.75
```

The results from the query are

```
[

        {"name":"Banana"},
        {"name":"Grapes"}

]
```

MongoDB API

With the MongoDB API, you can leverage your knowledge of MongoDB. In most cases, an existing MongoDB application would work without any code changes. All you need is to migrate your databases to an Azure Cosmos DB account that implements the MongoDB API, change the application's connection string, and that's it; it will be transparent for the application. In a sense, the application will think it is talking to MongoDB when in fact it is talking to Azure Cosmos DB.

The Azure portal also includes functionality so you can open a mongo shell where you can query your documents as you would with MongoDB.

Now, let's imagine you are a MongoDB developer building an application from scratch with .NET and will use Azure Cosmos DB to store your data. In order to leverage your existing knowledge so you can deliver your application faster, you will use the Mongo DB API SDK. You use the code in Listing 2-4 to initialize your client to talk to Azure Cosmos DB.

Listing 2-4. Initialization of the MongoDB API Client Using the
.NET SDK

```
var host = "host string shown in the Azure portal";
var dbName = "ProductCatalog";
var username = "jose";
var password = "p@sswOrd";
MongoClientSettings settings = new MongoClientSettings();
settings.Server = new MongoServerAddress(host, 10255);
settings.UseSsl = true;
settings.SslSettings = new SslSettings();
settings.SslSettings.EnabledSslProtocols = SslProtocols.Tls12;

MongoIdentity identity =
                    new MongoInternalIdentity(dbName, userName);
MongoIdentityEvidence evidence = new PasswordEvidence(password);

settings.Credentials = new List<MongoCredential>()
    {
        new MongoCredential("SCRAM-SHA-1", identity, evidence)
    };

MongoClient client = new MongoClient(settings);
```

The client configuration for an Azure Cosmos DB implementing
the MongoDB API has very strict networking rules. You start by creating
a `MongoClientSettings` object to configure how the client will be
connecting to the database. The configuration includes the host and port
as defined in the Azure portal for the Cosmos DB account. It is required to
use SSL and the TLS 1.2 protocol.

Next, you need to identify the application with a username and
password, and tell the API to which database you are connecting.

Now, to read the documents representing products in your database, use the code in Listing 2-5.

Listing 2-5. Getting the List of All Products

```
var collectionName = "Products";
var database = client.GetDatabase(dbName);
var prodCollection = database.GetCollection<Products>(collectionName);
var products = prodcollection.Find(new BsonDocument()).ToList();
```

From the code, you can see you are going to work in the ProductCatalog database, which contains a collection named Products. First, using the client object you get a reference to the database with the GetDatabase() method from the client object. Next, you read the collection with the GetCollection() method of the database object, and from there, get the list of products using a BsonDocument format.

Note   BSON is a binary-encoded serialization of a JSON document. BSON stands for Binary JSON. More information can be found at http://bsonspec.org/.

Graph API

A graph database, as opposed to a relational database, represents data as it exists in the real world, such as people, cars, computers, and so on, that are naturally connected, and does not try to change them in any way to define them as entities. Graphs are composed of *vertices* and *edges*. Both vertices and edges can have any number of properties. Vertices represent specific objects such as a person, place, or event. An edge is a relation between vertices.

For example, a vertex can be a person. Properties of this vertex are name, age, and gender. Another vertex is a phone. Properties of this vertex are brand and OS. An edge for these vertices could be "a person **uses** a phone." See this graph in Figure 2-14.

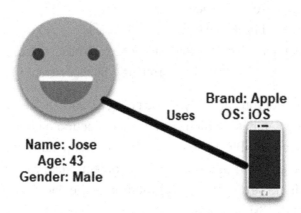

Figure 2-14. *A sample graph with two vertices and one edge*

Graphs are very useful to understand a wide range of datasets in different fields such as science and business. Graph databases let you work with graphs naturally and efficiently, and they typically are NoSQL because of their ability to adjust quickly to new or updated schemas. That's why implementing them in Azure Cosmos DB is a natural fit.

Graphs allow you to work with data in a powerful way by leveraging graph traversals found in many use cases and patterns because they outperform traditional SQL and NoSQL databases by several orders of magnitude. Also, they open the door to querying in a natural way of speaking, such as "find the names of the students who attended the Chicago Bulls basketball exhibition game last summer."

Azure Cosmos DB implements graph databases using the TinkerPop standard. You can use the Apache TinkerPop traversal language, Gremlin, or any other TinkerPop-compatible graph system like Apache Spark GraphX.

Listing 2-6 contains the code of a console application that implements the Azure Cosmos DB .NET SDK for Graph API. In the code, you first connect to an Azure Cosmos DB graph database account. For connecting, you need the end point, the primary or secondary key, and a connection policy. In this case, the connection policy, defined by a `ConnectionPolicy` object, specifies that the connection mode will be direct, which will connect the application directly to the data nodes in the Azure Cosmos DB account, and that the protocol will be TCP.

Next, you create a `DocumentClient` object inside a `using` statement to ensure it gets closed. The client object takes the endpoint parameter, the key, and connection policy.

Listing 2-6. Connecting and Querying an Azure Cosmos DB Graph Database Account

```
var endpoint = "https://productcatalog.documents.azure.com/dbs";
var authKey = "the primary or secondary key for the account";
var connPolicy = new ConnectionPolicy {
                    ConnectionMode = ConnectionMode.Direct,
                    ConnectionProtocol = Protocol.Tcp
              };
using (DocumentClient client = new DocumentClient(
              new Uri(endpoint),
              authKey,
              connPolicy)
{
      Database database = await
                    client.CreateDatabaseIfNotExistsAsync(
                        new Database { Id = "MyGraphDB" });
```

```csharp
DocumentCollection graph = await
        client.CreateDocumentCollectionIfNotExistsAsync(
            UriFactory.CreateDatabaseUri("MyGraphDB "),
            new DocumentCollection { Id = "MyColl" },
            new RequestOptions { OfferThroughput = 1000 });

IDocumentQuery<dynamic> query =
                    client.CreateGremlinQuery<dynamic>(
                            graph, "g.V().count()");

while (query.HasMoreResults)
{
    foreach (dynamic result in await query.ExecuteNextAsync())
    {
        Console.WriteLine($"\t
            {JsonConvert.SerializeObject(result)}");
    }
}
}
```

Using the client object, the code attempts to create a database named MyGraphDB, if it doesn't exist, with the method CreateDatabaseIfNotExistsAsync(). In the next line, it creates a new collection, if it doesn't exist already, called MyColl. The collection is configured with a throughput of 1,000 requests units per second.

The last part of the code is a Gremlin query that counts how many vertices are in the graph database and then prints the number out to the console.

Table API

An Azure Cosmos DB account implementing the Table API provides the same functionality as Azure Table storage but with the benefits of scalability and throughput from Cosmos DB. Another benefit (and difference) is that all properties are indexed, as opposed to Azure Table storage, which only indexes the PartitionKey and RowKey. Also, all five consistency models are available with the Azure Cosmos DB Table API versus only strong and eventual for Azure Table storage.

Listing 2-7 contains a small program that connects to an Azure Cosmos DB account implementing the Table API. The connection string is found in the Azure Cosmos DB account. First, you need to tell the SDK to which storage account it is connecting; you do so with a CloudStorageAccount object that takes the connection string as a parameter. You then create a CloudTableClient object, which is used to perform the operations against the database.

Using the cloud table client object, you obtain a reference to the products table using the method GetTableReference(), and it is stored in a CloudTable variable. If the table doesn't exists, it is created using the method CreateIfNotExists().

Listing 2-7. Connecting to an Azure Cosmos DB Account
Implementing the Table API Using the .NET SDK

```
CloudStorageAccount storageAccount =
                    CloudStorageAccount.Parse(connectionString);
CloudTableClient tableClient =
                    storageAccount.CreateCloudTableClient();
CloudTable table = tableClient.GetTableReference("products");
table.CreateIfNotExists();
ProductEntity item = new ProductEntity()
                     {
                            PartitionKey =
                                    Guid.NewGuid().ToString(),
                            RowKey = Guid.NewGuid().ToString(),
                            Name = $"Oranges",
                            Origin = "Florida"
                     };
TableOperation insertOperation = TableOperation.Insert(item);
table.Execute(insertOperation);
```

Next, a new product entity object is created and its properties filled. This object is passed as a parameter of a TableOperation object using the Insert() method. Using the table reference object, the operation object is passed as a parameter to the Execute() method, which effectively inserts the new item into the table.

Summary

In this chapter, you learned about the core concepts of Azure Cosmos DB. You started by understanding what global distribution is and how it helps take advantage of high availability and throughput by creating replicas of the databases across multiple Azure regions. Then you examined the different consistency models, their benefits, and when to use each one. You saw that most of the commercially available solutions only offer two consistency models, strong and eventual, but Azure Cosmos DB offers three more models that balance the requirements between availability and throughput. You then reviewed the concept of partitioning and why it is important. You studied the concept of containers and how they help the interaction between the application and the actual physical partitions by virtue of being a logical definition. You also viewed the considerations for partitioning and the criteria to choose the right partition key for the database.

The next concept was throughput. You saw that a request unit is a normalized number for all different data models based on the computational needs to execute an operation. This was necessary to provide a standard measure of calculating throughput and billing. You studied the different configurations for securing the databases starting from the storage with encryption at rest, the network with firewall capabilities, and access to data with master keys and resource tokens.

You finished the chapter by studying the different APIs that can be used to interact with Azure Cosmos DB. You reviewed each of them, starting from the core REST API and the implementations around it such as the DocumentDB API. You saw how existing MongoDB applications can work seamlessly with Azure Cosmos DB with virtually no changes to the application coding. Also, you studied the implementations of the Graph and Table APIs and their usage.

In the following chapter, I will dive in more detail into the operations around an Azure Cosmos DB database account using the DocumentDB API and the .NET SDK.

CHAPTER 3

Working with an Azure Cosmos DB Database

In this chapter, you will start working with a new Cosmos DB database. More specifically, it will be a database that implements the SQL DocumentDB API using the document data model. You will learn to use the DocumentDB API in a .NET application. You will create a database and collection with a partition key. Then you will learn how work with documents to create new documents and replace, delete, and query them. Finally, you will learn how to create and run stored procedures.

Your sample database will contain student records from a fictitious university named Cosmos University. You will be managing each student's record as they sign up for classes on a given year. The record will include information such as the name of the student, their postal addresses, email, and phone number. The intent of this database is to store the master record information of each student; therefore there won't be any information about their classes, professors, labs, or other related information.

© José Rolando Guay Paz 2018
J. R. Guay Paz, *Microsoft Azure Cosmos DB Revealed*,
https://doi.org/10.1007/978-1-4842-3351-1_3

Creating Your Database

Chapter 1 outlined the generic steps to create an Azure Cosmos DB database. Let's now create a real one. The following steps will guide you in creating one using the SQL DocumentDB API. To start creating a database, you will use the Azure Cosmos DB Emulator that you installed in Chapter 1. This will be a much easier environment to work with and, more importantly, you will not incur in any costs.

1. Open the Azure Cosmos DB Emulator by going to your browser and type in `https://localhost:8081/_explorer/index.html`, as shown in Figure 3-1.

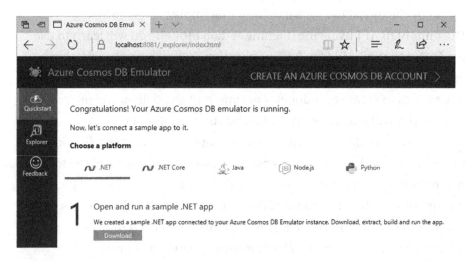

Figure 3-1. *Azure Cosmos DB Emulator home page*

2. It is possible that the emulator might not be running
    and you will get an error message similar to the one
    shown in Figure 3-2.

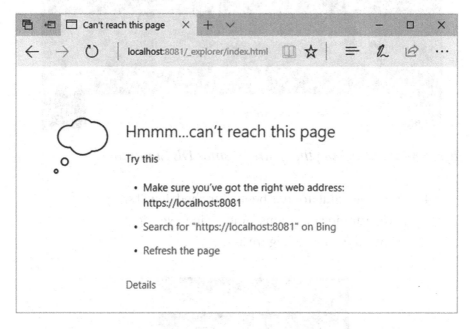

Figure 3-2. *Error message when the Azure Cosmos DB Emulator is
not running*

3. If you find the error shown in Figure 3-2, you need to
    launch the emulator. Click the Windows Start button
    and look for the Azure Cosmos DB Emulator folder.
    Expand the folder and click in the Azure Cosmos
    DB Emulator shortcut, as shown in Figure 3-3. You
    might see a notification in the lower right corner of
    your screen indicating that the emulator is starting.

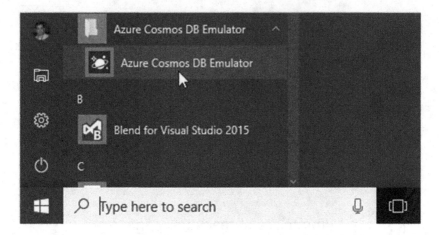

Figure 3-3. *Launching the Azure Cosmos DB Emulator*

4. Once the emulator has been launched, it will show
    in the running programs window in lower right
    corner, as shown in Figure 3-4.

Figure 3-4. *Azure Cosmos DB Emulator running*

5. With the emulator open, click the Explorer button in
    the left menu. Figure 3-5 shows the Explorer page.
    This is where you will create your database and
    collection.

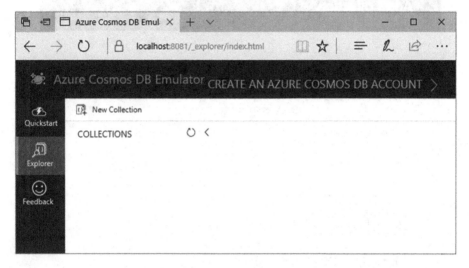

Figure 3-5. *The Explorer page from the Azure Cosmos DB Emulator*

6.   Click the New Collection button. Figure 3-6 shows
the new collection form. Note how this is similar to
the form shown in Figure 1-22 from Chapter 1.

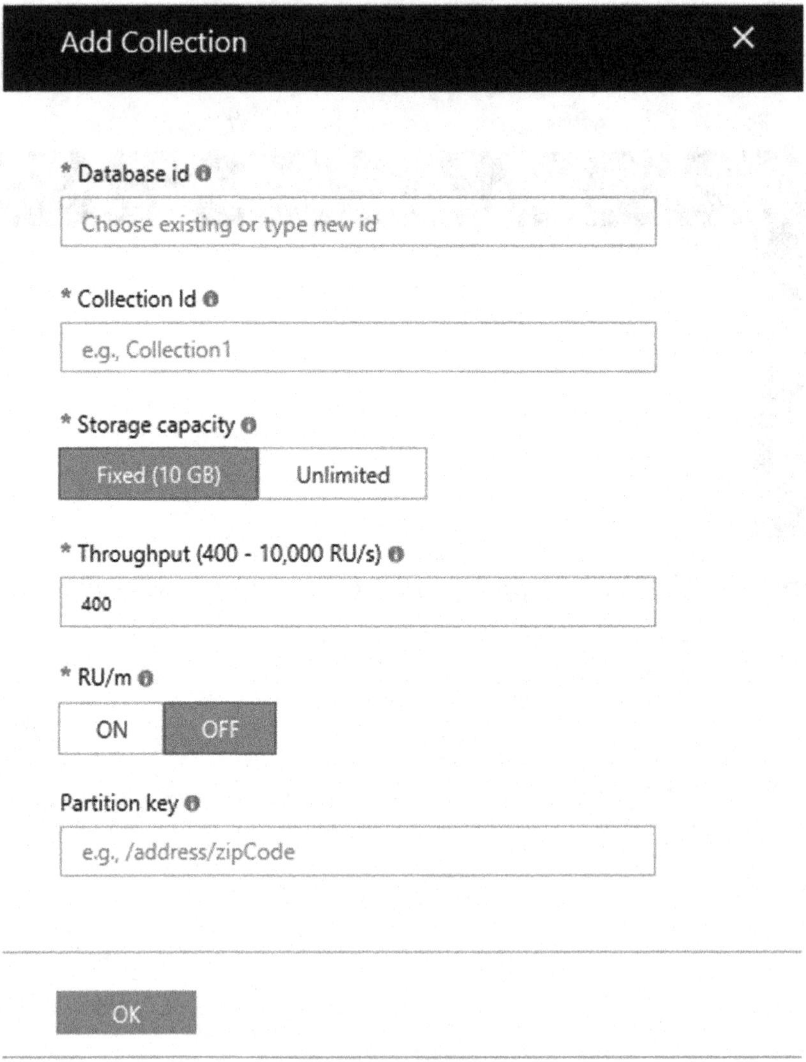

Add Collection   ✕

* Database id ⊕

Choose existing or type new id

* Collection Id ⊕

e.g., Collection1

* Storage capacity ⊕

| Fixed (10 GB) | Unlimited |

* Throughput (400 - 10,000 RU/s) ⊕

400

* RU/m ⊕

| ON | OFF |

Partition key ⊕

e.g., /address/zipCode

OK

Figure 3-6. *New collection window*

7. Let's start by typing the name of the database.
   The database name should be entered in
   lowercase letters in order to avoid problems when
   migrating to the actual Azure account and for an
   easier experience. For the database name, type
   `cosmosuniversity`.

8. In the following field, you need to type the name of
   the collection. Type `student`.

9. Then you select the type of storage: if it will be a
   fixed storage up to 10GB or unlimited. I discussed
   these parameters in Chapter 2. For your example,
   select *Unlimited*.

10. Now you need to select the throughput. Leave the
    default of *10,000* request units per second.

11. Finally, type the partition key for the collection. As
    mentioned in Chapter 2, this is a crucial element to
    achieve the expected throughput and to optimize
    the storage and utilization of the physical partitions.
    Let's use the *postal code* from the address. There
    are several thousand postal codes in the US alone,
    which will give us a good distribution. There might
    be a case, in the real world, where specific postal
    codes, such as the home town of the university,
    might introduce many more values than others, but
    it won't be the general rule. Type `/postalCode` in the
    partition key field.

12. In Figure 3-7 you can see the entire form completed.
     Click the OK button.

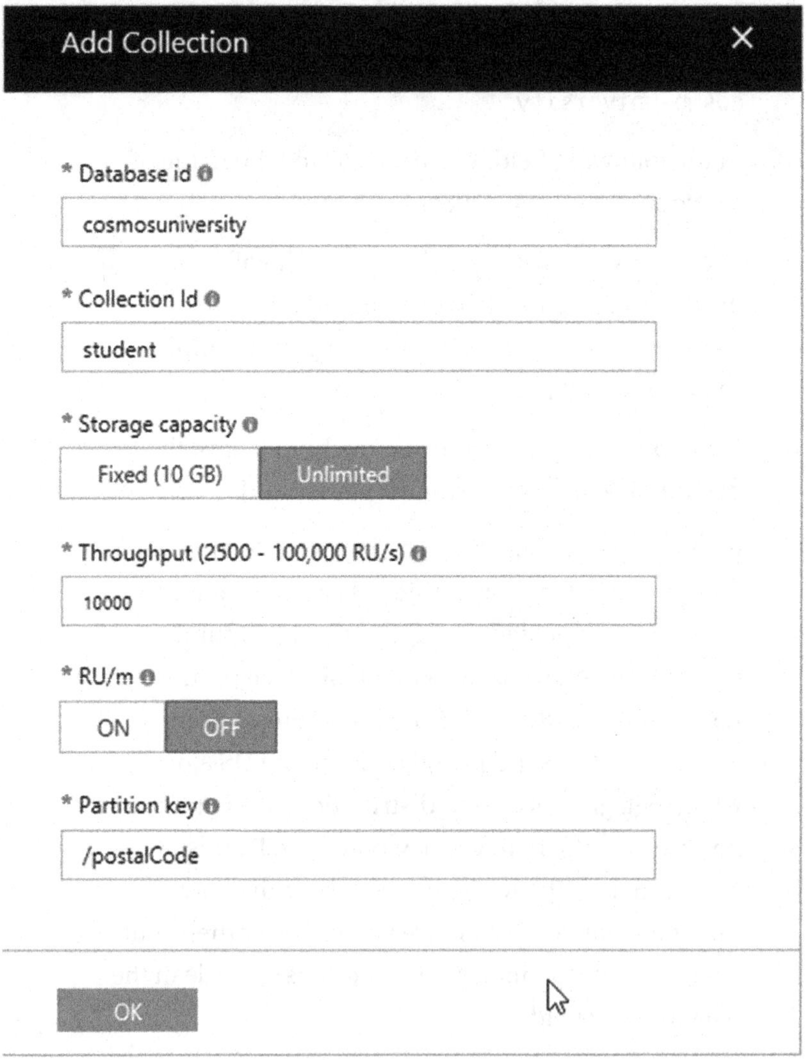

Figure 3-7. *New collection form filled with the required information*

13. After you click the OK button, the database
and collection will be created and you will see
something similar to Figure 3-8.

Figure 3-8. *Database and collection created in the Azure Cosmos
DB Emulator*

Defining the Document

Now that you have the collection ready, you need to define the document
that will represent the data. To represent the data, you will use JSON. JSON
stands for JavaScript Object Notation. It is a very lightweight and easy-to-
read-and-write data format. You can find more about JSON at www.json.org.

There are implementations of the JSON specification in nearly all
modern programming languages. The preferred and recommended
platform to work with JSON documents in .NET is Json.NET by Newtonsoft
(www.newtonsoft.com/json); in fact, Microsoft updated the Visual Studio
templates to use Json.NET instead of the .NET implementation in the
System.Json serialization namespace.

Since the document will store information about student records, you
will have something similar to Listing 3-1. In the listing, what you see is a
definition using JSON to format the information.

Listing 3-1. Student Record Definition in JSON

```
{
        "id": "1",
        "firstName": "Jose",
        "lastName": "Guay",
        "birthDate": "04/07/1974",
        "address1": "1234 Main Street",
        "address2": "",
        "city": "Chicago",
        "state": "IL",
        "postalCode": 60601,
        "phoneNumber": "312-123-4567"
}
```

The listing shows the property id as a string. While in this example it is a number, automatically generated ids in Azure Cosmos DB are GUIDs stored as strings. The properties firstName, lastName, and phoneNumber are strings. The property birthDate is a date. The properties address1, address2, city, and state from the mail address are strings and, finally, postalCode is an integer.

The document definition in Listing 3-1 will help you get through the remainder of this chapter, and you will modify it in future chapters as you dive into different topics of the implementation.

Managing Documents

There are several ways to manage documents using Azure Cosmos DB. The easiest is to use the emulator or Azure portal interface to query and manipulate them. This method is, however, only useful for administrators or developers. The most common method for end users is to use an application built for this purpose. Finally, for the bulk import scenario there is a tool called Data Migration Tool that can take information from a source and import it into an Azure Cosmos DB database.

In this chapter, you will use the emulator so you can get started right away creating, modifying, and deleting documents. You will then implement a small web application that will facilitate these tasks for end users. I will address the Data Migration Tool in Chapter 4.

Using the Azure Cosmos DB Emulator to Manage Documents

Now that you have a database and collection created, you will start using the Azure Cosmos DB Emulator to manipulate documents. The emulator's interface is remarkably similar to the Azure portal interface. This was done on purpose so that you can learn once and use everywhere. Follow the next steps to work with the emulator:

1. With the database and collection open as shown in Figure 3-8, click the arrow to the left of the collection name to expand the options. Figure 3-9 shows the different elements you can work with in the collection. This list will give you the ability to not only work with documents but also to change the scalability and settings configuration and manage stored procedures, user defined functions, and triggers.

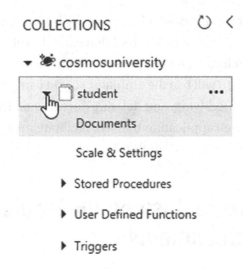

Figure 3-9. *Expanding the collection options*

2. Click the Documents option. You will see a new set of options on the screen, as shown in Figure 3-10. The page now gives you two toolbars, one at the top of the page with buttons to create different elements in the database such as a new query, new stored procedure, new user defined function, and new trigger. You can also create a new collection or delete the current collection.

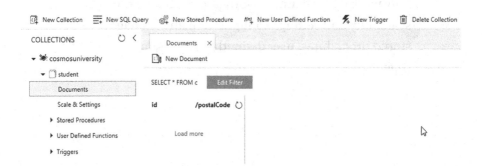

Figure 3-10. *Options on the Documents page*

The second toolbar is specific to documents and
it is in a new tab to the right of the page. Inside the
tab, the second toolbar has only a single button at
this point, to create a new document. Note in the
Documents tab the SQL query that is use to read
information from the collection. Below the query
the page is divided in two sections. To the left is a
pane with two columns: one for the value of the id
in the document and the second for the value of the
partition key. In the right-side pane, you will be able
to see and manipulate the documents. Once you have
documents, the toolbar will show more buttons.

3. Click the New Document button to create a new
    document that will be inserted into the database.
    You will see a starting JSON document like the one in
    Figure 3-11. This is a skeleton document that you can
    use to start typing your document values. Also note
    that two new buttons showed up in the toolbar: one to
    save your document and one to discard the new record.

Figure 3-11. *Adding a new document*

4. You will now copy the document from Listing 3-1 into the new document pane, completely replacing the skeleton document. It will look like Figure 3-12. Then click the Save button.

Figure 3-12. *New document using the information from Listing 3-1*

5. After you click the Save button, the page changes a little bit. As shown in Figure 3-13, the value of the id field and the value of the partition key are showing in the left-side list, and the toolbar shows different buttons. You now have a button to delete the document and two buttons to save or discard modifications.

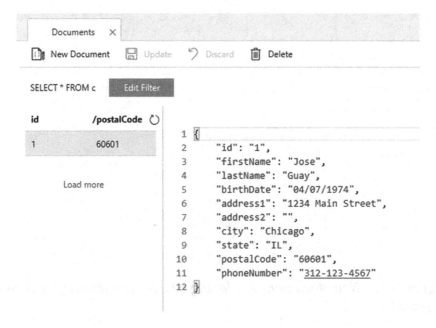

Figure 3-13. *New document saved in the collection*

6. If you click the row in the left pane referencing the
    new document, as shown in Figure 3-14, you will
    see the document reloads but it has been modified a
    little bit. It has new properties that were not present
    in Listing 3-1. These properties were added by Azure
    Cosmos DB. The new properties are described in
    Table 3-1.

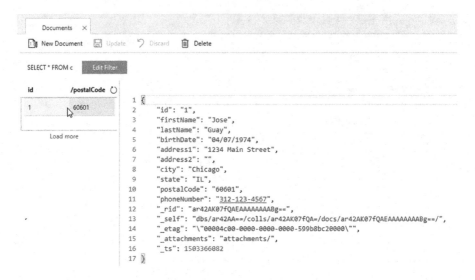

Figure 3-14. *New document displaying new properties used by Azure Cosmos DB*

Table 3-1. *Internal Properties in Azure Cosmos DB Documents (source: http://bit.ly/cosmos-db-create-doc)*

Property	Description
_rid	This is a system-generated property. The resource ID (_rid) is a unique identifier that is also hierarchical per the resource stack on the resource model. It is used internally for placement and navigation of the document resource.
_self	This is a system-generated property. It is the unique addressable URI for the resource.
_etag	This is a system-generated property that specifies the resource etag required for optimistic concurrency control.
_attachments	This is a system-generated property that specifies the addressable path for the attachments resource.
_ts	This is a system-generated property. It specifies the last updated timestamp of the resource. The value is a timestamp.

7. To modify the value of a document, all you need to do is adjust it in the right pane and click the Update button.

8. To delete a document, just select the document from the left-side list and click the Delete button.

Managing Documents with an Application

You will now build a small web application using Visual Studio 2017 to manage documents. This is a different scenario, targeted to end users, in which you will use the .NET SDK to interact with the database and collection that you created in the Azure Cosmos DB Emulator.

Creating the ASP.NET Web Application

The following steps will guide you through the process of developing this web application:

1. Open Visual Studio 2017 from the Start menu, as shown in Figure 3-15.

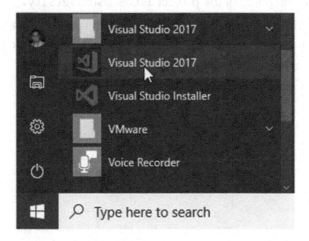

Figure 3-15. *Open Visual Studio 2017 from the Start menu*

2. Go to the *File* menu, select *New*, and from the menu
    select *Project*. As shown in Figure 3-16, you can also
    use the keyboard shortcut of Ctrl-Shift-N.

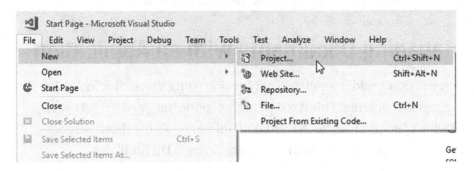

Figure 3-16. *Creating a new project in Visual Studio 2017*

3. The new project window is shown in Figure 3-17. You
    now have the option to create any type of application.
    From the list of templates in the left, select *Web*, and
    from the options in the center pane, select *ASP.NET
    Web Application (.NET Framework)*. At the bottom,
    type the name of the project as CosmosUniversity.
    Web. Select a folder where the application files will be
    saved and make sure the *Create directory for solution*
    checkbox is selected in the lower right corner of the
    window. Then click the OK button.

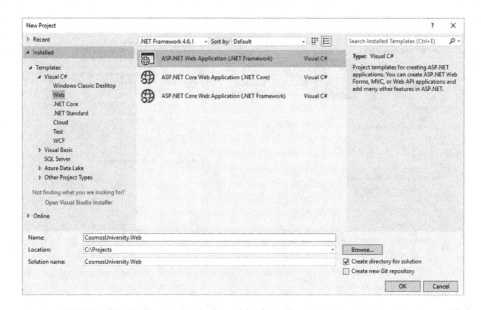

Figure 3-17. *New ASP.NET web application*

4. A new window opens to select the type template for your web application. Select *MVC* to create a new ASP.NET MVC web application, as shown in Figure 3-18. Leave the default authentication configuration, which is *No Authentication*, and don't select the option to create a unit tests project. Then click the OK button.

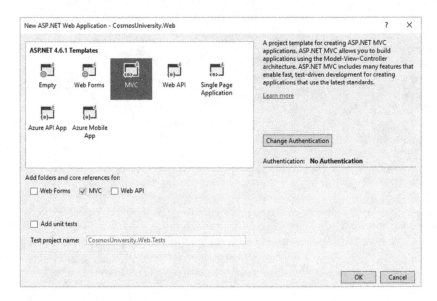

Figure 3-18. *Options to create a new ASP.NET web application*

Note   In a real application, you would want to implement authentication and unit tests. Unit tests will help you evaluate your code as you develop and will potentially identify breaking changes whenever new code is introduced. Depending on the requirements of your application, authentication will play an important role in identifying and authorizing users for different actions. For the purpose of this sample application, these two features are not needed because I only want to illustrate working with the Azure Cosmos DB database.

---

5. Visual Studio will now start creating all the necessary files based on the template and the options selected, as shown in Figure 3-19.

Figure 3-19. *Visual Studio progress window when creating the new ASP.NET web application*

6. Once the application has been created, Visual Studio will show the Solution Explorer window shown in Figure 3-20.

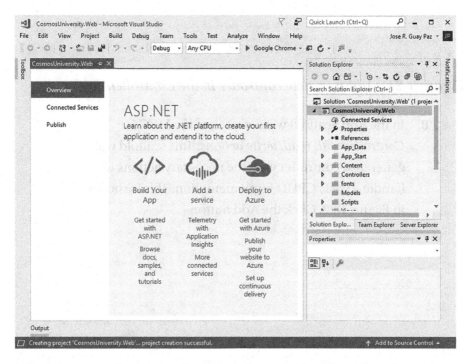

Figure 3-20. *Solution Explorer window in Visual Studio after the new ASP.NET web application is created*

81

7. Next, you will create the controller to handle
    the application's interaction with the user and
    coordinate what needs to happen on each action.
    Right-click in the `Controllers` folder and from the
    context menu select *Add* and then *Controller*, as
    shown in Figure 3-21.

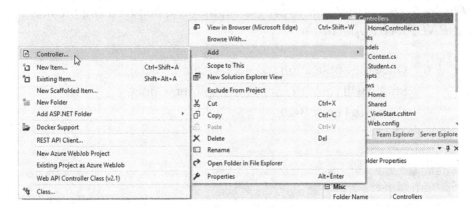

Figure 3-21. *Adding a new controller in the Controllers folder*

8. In the Add Scaffold window, select *the MVC 5
    Controller with read/write actions.* This scaffold will
    generate a controller with the necessary actions to
    handle a basic CRUD implementation. This is shown
    in Figure 3-22. Click the Add button.

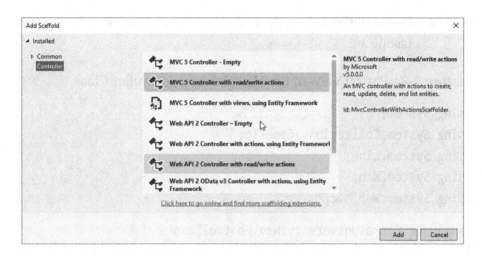

Figure 3-22. *Adding a scaffold window and creating a controller with read/write actions*

9. In the Add Controller window, shown in
    Figure 3-23, the name of the controller should be
    StudentController.

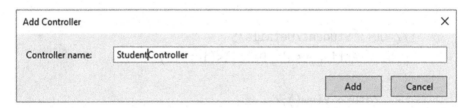

Figure 3-23. *Configuring the new controller name as StudentController*

10.   Part of the code from the new controller is shown in
      Listing 3-2.

Listing 3-2. Partial View of the New StudentController Class

```
using System;
using System.Collections.Generic;
using System.Linq;
using System.Web;
using System.Web.Mvc;

namespace CosmosUniversity.Web.Controllers
{
    public class StudentController : Controller
    {
        // GET: Student
        public ActionResult Index()
        {
            return View();
        }

        // GET: Student/Details/5
        public ActionResult Details(int id)
        {
            return View();
        }

        // GET: Student/Create
        public ActionResult Create()
        {
            return View();
        }
```

```
// POST: Student/Create
[HttpPost]
public ActionResult Create(FormCollection collection)
{
    try
    {
        // TODO: Add insert logic here

        return RedirectToAction("Index");
    }
    catch
    {
        return View();
    }
}
```

...

Creating a Class for the Document

It is time to create a structure that you can manipulate for the data. Since you are using .NET and C#, you will create a new class that represents a document in the database. It will contain all the properties necessary to match the document in Listing 3-1. This will be your document model. Using a class will be much easier than manipulating JSON directly, and in the end, you will use Json.net to serialize this class into the actual JSON document. Follow the next steps to create the document:

1.   Right-click in the Models folder in the Solution Explorer window. From the context menu, select *Add* and then *Class,* as shown in Figure 3-24.

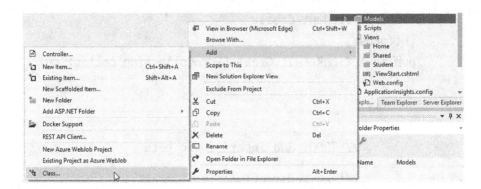

Figure 3-24. *Adding a new class in the Models folder for your document*

2. When the Add New Item window opens, type the name of the file as `Student.cs` and click the Add button, as shown in Figure 3-25.

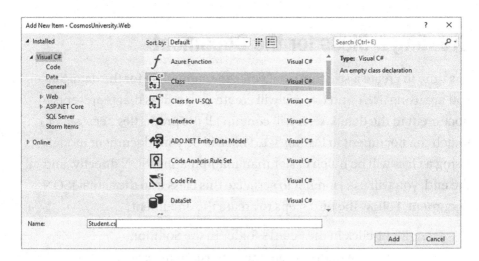

Figure 3-25. *Creating a new class named Student.cs that represents a record in the database*

3. The class at this point will be empty. Let's now
    add properties representing each of the properties
    described in the JSON document from Listing 3-1.
    These properties are shown in Listing 3-3.

Listing 3-3. Student Model Representing a Record in the Database

```
using System;
using System.Collections.Generic;
using System.Linq;
using System.Web;

namespace CosmosUniversity.Web.Models
{
    public class Student
    {
        public string Id { get; set; }
        public string FirstName { get; set; }
        public string LastName { get; set; }
        public DateTime BirthDate { get; set; }
        public string Address1 { get; set; }
        public string Address2 { get; set; }
        public string City { get; set; }
        public string State { get; set; }
        public int PostalCode { get; set; }
        public string PhoneNumber { get; set; }
    }
}
```

Note that the names of the properties in the class use Pascal Case notation while the JSON document uses Camel Case. This might cause some problems but they are easily solved by adding annotations to match the casing between both formats. To make these annotations you will need to add the Newtonsoft.Json namespace to the class and use the [JsonProperty] attribute on each property, as shown in Listing 3-4.

Listing 3-4. Student Model Now with Annotations in the Class Properties to Match the JSON Document's Camel Case Style

```
using Newtonsoft.Json;
using System;
using System.Collections.Generic;
using System.Linq;
using System.Web;

namespace CosmosUniversity.Web.Models
{
    public class Student
    {
        [JsonProperty(PropertyName = "id")]
        public string Id { get; set; }

        [JsonProperty(PropertyName = "firstName")]
        public string FirstName { get; set; }

        [JsonProperty(PropertyName = "lastName")]
        public string LastName { get; set; }

        [JsonProperty(PropertyName = "birthDate")]
        public DateTime BirthDate { get; set; }

        [JsonProperty(PropertyName = "address1")]
        public string Address1 { get; set; }
```

```
    [JsonProperty(PropertyName = "address2")]
    public string Address2 { get; set; }

    [JsonProperty(PropertyName = "city")]
    public string City { get; set; }

    [JsonProperty(PropertyName = "state")]
    public string State { get; set; }

    [JsonProperty(PropertyName = "postalCode")]
    public int PostalCode { get; set; }

    [JsonProperty(PropertyName = "phoneNumber")]
    public string PhoneNumber { get; set; }
  }
}
```

Creating the Data Layer

The web application is now ready for you to create the data layer. This will be a class that implements the integration between the web application and Azure Cosmos DB. The first thing you need to do is let the application know you want to use Azure Cosmos DB, and for that you need to add a new library to the solution. You will use a NuGet package for that. The following steps will guide you through the creation of the data layer class:

1. The first step is to add the DocumentDB .NET SDK to the project. To do so, open the NuGet Package Manager Console. The console is a command line interface where you can type the commands to install, update, or remove a package from the projects in a solution. To use it, go to the *Tools* menu, open *NuGet Package Manager*, and then select *Package Manager Console*, as shown in Figure 3-26.

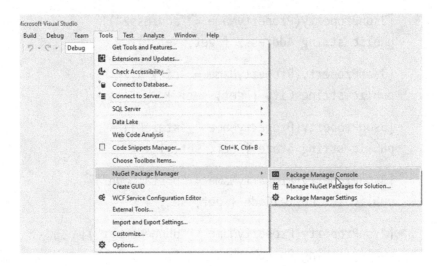

Figure 3-26. *Opening the Package Manager Console window*

2. The Package Manager Console window is shown in Figure 3-27. At this point, you can enter package commands.

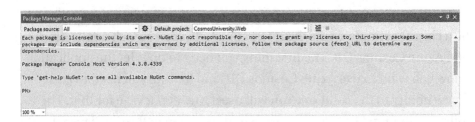

Figure 3-27. *Package Manager Console window*

3. A graphical user interface for managing packages is available in case you are not too comfortable with the command line interface. The option, shown in Figure 3-28, is available just below the Package Manager Console in the Tools menu and is called Manage NuGet Packages for Solution.

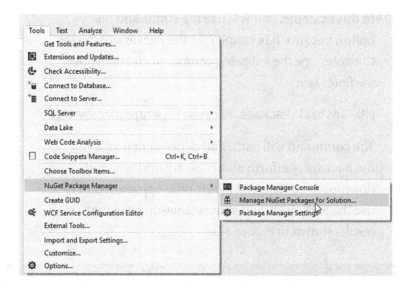

Figure 3-28. *Opening the graphical user interface to manage packages*

4. The graphical user interface for managing packages
   is shown in Figure 3-29.

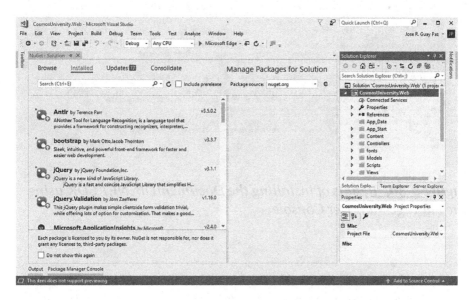

Figure 3-29. *Graphical user interface to manage packages*

5.   In this example, you will use the command line
     option because it is simpler. In the Package Manager
     Console, type the following command and then press
     the Enter key:

```
PM> Install-Package Microsoft.Azure.DocumentDB
```

6.   The command will gather all dependencies for
     the package, perform all necessary updates, and
     download the required files for the application to
     use the SDK. It should show something like the
     results shown in Figure 3-30.

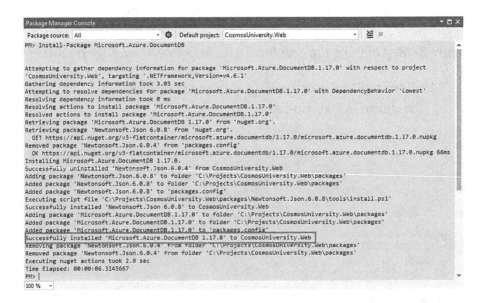

Figure 3-30. *Results of installing the DocumentDB .NET SDK using
the Package Manager Console*

7. Let's now start writing some code. For your
    application to connect to Azure Cosmos DB it
    needs two pieces of information: it needs to know
    where the database is and it needs to know the
    authentication key. The location of the database is
    information you saw in Chapter 1. It is basically the
    URL where the emulator is running. The second
    piece is a fixed authentication key for the emulator
    that never changes and is intended to be used only
    with it; it can't be used for production databases in
    Microsoft Azure. The values are

```
Database endpoint URL: https://localhost:8081/
Authentication Key: C2y6yDjf5/R+obON8A7Cgv30VRD
JIWEHLM+4QDU5DE2nQ9nDuVTqobD4b8mGGyPMbIZnqyMsEc
aGQy67XIw/Jw==
```

8. Add these values to the Web.Config file so they are
    easy to use in the application. Open the Web.Config
    file in Visual Studio and add the following lines in
    the <AppSettings> section as shown in Figure 3-31.
    Then save the file and close it.

```
<add key="CosmodDBEndPoint"
value="https://localhost:8081/"/>
<add key="CosmosDBAuthKey" value="C2y6yDjf5/R+
obON8A7Cgv30VRDJIWEHLM+4QDU5DE2nQ9nDuVTqobD4b8mG
GyPMbIZnqyMsEcaGQy67XIw/Jw=="/>
```

```
Web.config*  ⊕ X
    1   <?xml version="1.0" encoding="utf-8"?>
    2   <!--
    3     For more information on how to configure your ASP.NET application, please visit
    4     https://go.microsoft.com/fwlink/?LinkId=301880
    5     -->
    6   <configuration>
    7     <configSections>
    8       <section name="entityFramework" type="System.Data.Entity.Internal.ConfigFile.EntityFrameworkSection, EntityFramework, Version=6.0
    9     </configSections>
   10     <appSettings>
   11       <add key="webpages:Version" value="3.0.0.0" />
   12       <add key="webpages:Enabled" value="false" />
   13       <add key="ClientValidationEnabled" value="true" />
   14       <add key="UnobtrusiveJavaScriptEnabled" value="true" />
   15       <add key="CosmodDBEndPoint" value="https://localhost:8081/"/>
   16       <add key="CosmosDBAuthKey" value="C2y6yDjf5/R+ob0NBA7Cgv30VRDJIWEHLM+4QDU5DE2nQ9nDuVTqobD4b8mGGyPNbIZnqyMsEcaGQy67XIw/Jw=="/>
   17     </appSettings>
```

Figure 3-31.   *The Web.Config file after adding the two keys for connecting to the Azure Cosmos DB Emulator*

Note   More information on the Azure Cosmos DB Emulator can be found in Chapter 1 and throughout this book and in the online documentation at `http://bit.ly/cosmos-db-emulator`.

---

9. In the same way you added a class for the document, let's create a new class for the data layer. Right-click the Models folder, open *Add* from the context menu, and select *Class* at the bottom, as shown in Figure 3-24. When the Add New Item window opens, as shown in Figure 3-32, type the name of the new class as Repository.cs.

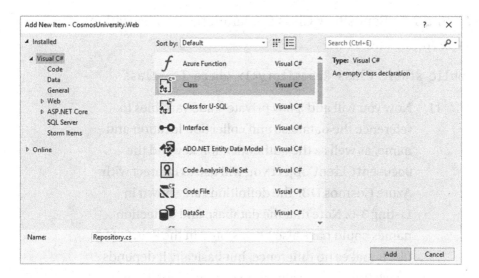

Figure 3-32. *Creating the new Repository class for the data layer*

10.   You will change the default class code in several
       ways to facilitate accessing it. First, you will make the
       class static so that you don't have to create instances
       of it. Also, you will constraint your class to be able
       to work only with class type arguments. This is
       important because you are effectively saying that the
       data layer will work only with classes such as the one
       you built for the student records. Note that this refers
       to any class, not just the Student class, and thus, it
       can work with more class types as you add them. The
       new class declaration is shown in Listing 3-5.

Listing 3-5. Repository Class Declaration with Restrictions for Class Type Arguments

```
public static class Repository<T> where T : class
```

11. Now you will add a few private static variables to reference the database and collection location and name, as well as the authentication key and the DocumentClient object you will use to interact with Azure Cosmos DB. The definitions are shown in Listing 3-6. Note that the database and collection names could have also been stored in the Web.Config file. It makes no difference, but basically it depends on whether those values can change in the future or not, and how easily you want them to update.

Listing 3-6. Private Variables to Store Global Information to the Repository Class

```
private static readonly string _endPoint =
        ConfigurationManager.AppSettings["CosmosDBEndPoint"];
private static readonly string _authKey =
        ConfigurationManager.AppSettings["CosmosDBAuthKey"];
private static readonly string _dbName = "cosmosuniversity";
private static readonly string _collectionName = "student";
private static readonly DocumentClient =
            new DocumentClient(new Uri(_endPoint), _authKey);
```

Querying the Database

You are ready to start querying the database. To make it very responsive, you will add an `async` method that returns a list of students; that way the application UI won't be locked while the query is executing.

The code for the method is shown in Listing 3-7. The method will accept as a parameter a lambda expression that can be used to filter and refine the query.

Listing 3-7. Async Method to Query the Azure Cosmos DB Collection to Read All the Student Documents

```
public static async Task<IEnumerable<T>>
                GetStudentsAsync(Expression<Func<T, bool>> where)
{
    Uri collectionUri = UriFactory.CreateDocumentCollectionUri
                                    (_dbName, _collectionName);
    FeedOptions feedOptions = new FeedOptions { MaxItemCount = -1 };
    IDocumentQuery<T> students;

    if (where == null)
    {
        students = client.CreateDocumentQuery<T>
                                (collectionUri, feedOptions)
                            .AsDocumentQuery();
    }
    else
```

```
    {
        students = client.CreateDocumentQuery<T>
                                    (collectionUri, feedOptions)
                                    .Where(where)
                                    .AsDocumentQuery();
    }

    List<T> listOfStudents = new List<T>();
    while (students.HasMoreResults)
    {
        listOfStudents.AddRange(await students.ExecuteNextAsync<T>());
    }

    return listOfStudents;
}
```

The first line creates an `Uri` variable. This variable will store the actual link used to connect to the collection. It is built using the `CreateDocumentCollectionUri` function in the `UriFactory` class and takes as a parameter the name of the database and the name of the collection to which you want to connect.

The second line creates a new `FeedOptions` variable which is used to provide the client object with information about how to return results from queries. In this example, by setting the `MaxItemCount` to `-1`, you're telling the client to dynamically calculate the page size. For example, a value of 10 for this property would instruct the client to return 10 documents at a time. The `FeedOptions` class has many properties to configure the client, such as `PartitionKey` which defines the partition key to use in the case of an operation involving a specific partition. `SessionToken` gets or sets the session token for use with Session consistency.

The following line creates an IDocumentQuery variable. It will be used to read the information from the database and collection specified in the Uri passed in the first parameter, and it will use the configuration in the FeedOptions variable from the second parameter. The next line adds a Where() extension for the query that in turn uses the expression in the GetStudentsAsync method's parameter as a predicate to filter the results. Finally, since the Where() extension returns an IQueryable, you need to convert this result to an IDocumentQuery and you use the extension AsDocumentQuery(). Note that because the Where() extension requires the predicate not to be null, you are checking if this is the case, and if so, it will not add the extension to the query.

The final lines of the method create a List<T> to store the results from the DocumentQuery. The query is executed page by page and you need to loop through all the pages of data. The property HasMoreResults from the DocumentQuery object is a Boolean that will be true if there are more results to read. The first time it's checked, it will return true; it then enters the while loop and adds to the list of results the documents returned from the call to ExecuteNextAsync<T>(). This method will go to the collection, read the next page of data, and if there are more documents to read, based on the query, it will keep the value of true for HasMoreResults. When there are no more results to read, HasMoreResults becomes false and the loop ends. Then the method finishes, returning a list of students.

To read a single document, you access it using its id. Listing 3-8 shows the method GetStudentAsync() (note that the name is singular this time). The method accepts as a parameter the id of the student you want to see.

Listing 3-8. Async Method to Query the Azure Cosmos DB Collection to Read a Student Document Based on Its Id

```
public static async Task<T> GetStudentAsync(string id)
{
```

```
if (string.IsNullOrEmpty(id))
    throw new ApplicationException("No student id specified");

Uri documentUri = UriFactory.CreateDocumentUri
                            (_dbName, _collectionName, id);
try
{
    Document student =
                await client.ReadDocumentAsync(documentUri);
    return (T)(dynamic)student;
}
catch (DocumentClientException ex)
{
    if (ex.StatusCode == System.Net.HttpStatusCode.NotFound)
        return null;

    throw;
}
}
```

The first two lines in the method are a validation to ensure you are getting an actual value to query the database. It is a simple defensive mechanism to avoid a roundtrip to the database that most surely will fail and will just consume RUs.

The following line creates an Uri object that identifies the document in the collection. The three parameters are the database, collection, and id of the document. The UriFactory.CreateDocumentUri() method will make sure the Uri is properly created.

To read the document you use the client.ReadDocumentAsync() method. The way this method works is if the document is found, then it returns the document; otherwise, it throws an exception of type DocumentClientException. Documents either exist or not; therefore, if the document is not found, the status code for the exception will be an HttpStatusCode.NotFound. In this case, the method will just return null.

You use a `try-catch` statement to check for this exception. In the rare case where something else happens, the method will just rethrow the exception so it is visible and can be addressed. Converting the document to a `dynamic` object and then casting to T will easily and implicitly take care of the deserialization from JSON to object using the type represented by T.

Creating a Document

Creating a document using the DocumentDB .NET SDK is a very simple process. Once you have an object that maps to the document being stored in the collection, you use the `client.CreateDocumentAsync()` method, as shown in Listing 3-9.

Listing 3-9. Async Method to Connect to the Azure Cosmos DB Collection to Create a New Student Document

```
public static async Task<Document> CreateStudentAsync(T student)
{
    Uri collectionUri = UriFactory.CreateDocumentCollectionUri
                                      (_dbName, _collectionName);
    return await client.CreateDocumentAsync(collectionUri, student);
}
```

The first line creates the Uri for the collection so the method knows to which collection you are referring to when creating the document. The Uri takes two parameters, the database and collection you intend to connect to. The second line is the call to `client.CreateDocumentAsync()` that takes two parameters: the first one is the Uri created before, and the second is the document to be created.

Replacing a Document

When a document changes and those changes are saved to the database, it is called a replace operation. This is done using the client.ReplaceDocumentAsync() method shown in Listing 3-10.

Listing 3-10. Async Method to Connect to the Azure Cosmos DB Collection to Replace a Student Document

```
public static async Task<Document> ReplaceStudentAsync
                                        (T student, string id)
{
    if (string.IsNullOrEmpty(id))
        throw new ApplicationException("No student id specified");

    Uri documentUri = UriFactory.CreateDocumentUri
                            (_dbName, _collectionName, id);
    return await client.ReplaceDocumentAsync(documentUri, student);
}
```

The method will accept two parameters: the document with the new values and the id of the document. The document id will be used to create the Uri of the document in the first line. The second line is the call to client.ReplaceDocumentAsync() which connects to the collection and replaces the document. As usual, you check the id variable to ensure there is a value and throw an exception if there isn't one.

Deleting a Document

Deleting a document is done by calling the client.DeleteDocumentAsync() method which accepts a single parameter: the Uri of the document you intend to delete. Listing 3-11 shows the method to delete a student document.

Listing 3-11. Async Method to Connect to the Azure Cosmos DB
Collection to Delete a Student Document

```
public static async Task<Document> DeleteStudentAsync(string id)
{
    if (string.IsNullOrEmpty(id))
        throw new ApplicationException("No student id specified");

    Uri documentUri = UriFactory.CreateDocumentUri
                                (_dbName, _collectionName, id);
    return await client.DeleteDocumentAsync(documentUri);
}
```

Using the Data Layer in the Controller and Completing the Application

It is now time to implement the data layer and add the necessary code in
the controller so you can interact with Azure Cosmos DB.

The first step to implement is the list of students. The idea is that
when a user opens the Students page they will get the list of students to
manipulate. The page will have the list of students, an option to create a
new student, and options to view, edit, and delete individual documents.
The following steps will guide you through the adjustments to the
StudentController class:

1. Open the StudentController.cs file by
    double-clicking it in the Solution Explorer window,
    as shown in Figure 3-33.

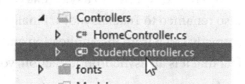

Figure 3-33. *Opening the StudentController.cs file*

2. In the Index() action, add the code to call the GetStudentsAsync() method from Repository. The code will look similar to what is shown in Listing 3-12.

Listing 3-12. Calling GetStudentsAsync()

```
var students = await Repository<Student>.GetStudentsAsync(null);
return View(students);
```

3. After you add the code you will notice a problem highlighted with a red squiggle, as shown in Figure 3-34. The issue here is that you are trying to call an asynchronous function from a synchronous method.

```
public class StudentController : Controller
{
    // GET: Student
    public ActionResult Index()
    {
        var students = await Repository<Student>.GetStudentsAsync(null);
        return View(students);
    }
}
```

Figure 3-34. *Issue when calling an asynchronous function from a synchronous method*

4. To resolve this problem, you must adjust the action so that it is also asynchronous. Instead of this being a simple ActionResult method, it should be changed to be a Task<ActionResult> and it also needs to be modified to be async. To keep it consistent with the convention of async-await, the action is also renamed to IndexAsync(). Finally, in order to correctly call it from the application and hide the fact that it is an asynchronous action, you

decorate the action with an annotation so its name is known as just Index. The resulting code is in Listing 3-13.

Listing 3-13. Modified Controller Action to Become Asynchronous

```
[ActionName("Index")]
public async Task<ActionResult> IndexAsync()
{
    var students = await Repository<Student>.GetStudentsAsync(null);
    return View(students);
}
```

5. You now add the view to render the list of students. In the IndexAsync() action, right-click anywhere inside the action and at the top of the context menu you will see an option named *Add View*, as shown in Figure 3-35. This will open the Add View window shown in Figure 3-36. In the Add View window, type the name of the view as Index only so it matches the actual action name and follows the MVC convention. Then select the List template. The Model class should be the Student class in the Models folder. Then click the Add button.

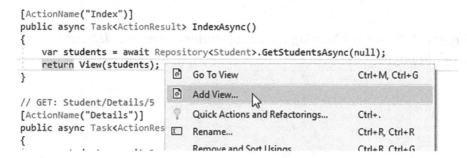

Figure 3-35. *Adding a view for the action method*

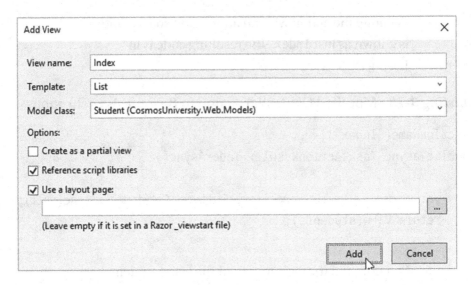

Figure 3-36. *The Add View window with the configuration to create a list of items*

6. Once you compile and run the application, just type in the URL generated for the Student controller (/Student) and you will see something like Figure 3-37.

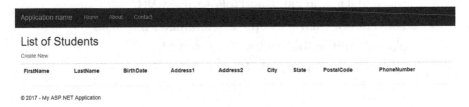

Figure 3-37. *Page showing the list of students with the default scaffold page*

7. The rest of the actions in the controller must also be adjusted to be asynchronous. As you did before, the modifications are as follows:

   a. `ActionResult` becomes `Task<ActionResult>`.

   b. The `async` modifier is added.

   c. The method is renamed to end with `Async`.

   d. An annotation is added so the action name is not the same as the action method.

8. The code for the `Details()` action is similar to the one in Listing 3-13. The difference is that instead of returning a list of students it will return a single one. The `id` parameter also needs to be adjusted so it is a `string`. The resulting code is in Listing 3-14.

Listing 3-14. Action to Read a Single Student Document

```
[ActionName("Details")]
public async Task<ActionResult> DetailsAsync(string id)
{
    var student = await Repository<Student>.GetStudentAsync(id);
    return View(student);
}
```

9. Now, similarly to what you did before, let's add the view for this action. Right-click in any part of the action and select *Add View*. In the Add View window type the name of the view as `Details`, the template should be Details, and the Model class will be again Student. The window is shown in Figure 3-38.

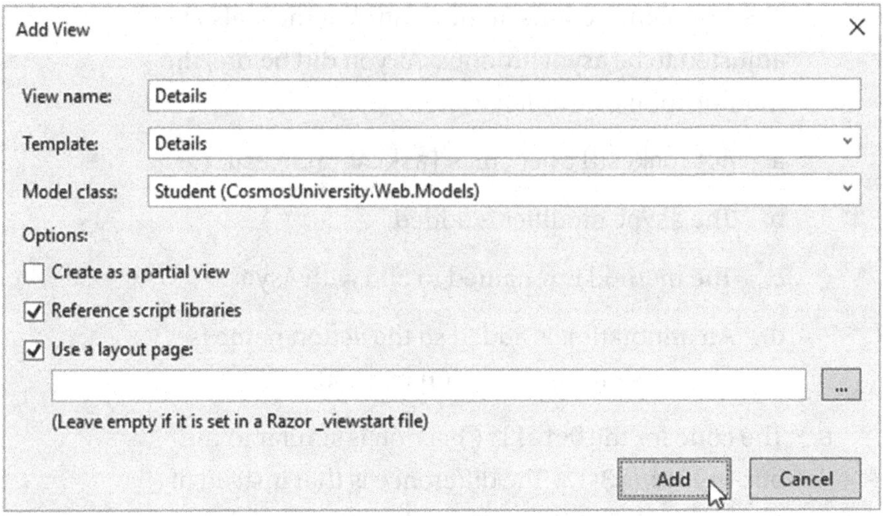

Figure 3-38. *Adding the view for the viewing the details of a Student document*

10. You are now going to write the code to create documents. You need two actions this time: one for the empty form so the user can enter the information of the new document, and one action that will receive the information and store it in Azure Cosmos DB. You will see those two actions in the controller; one is a simple `ActionResult` method named `Create()` and the other has an annotation that restricts its usage to just respond to `POST` requests. Leave the first method as is; you don't need to change it to be asynchronous because it will just serve the form to enter the information, but the second one must be adjusted to become `async`. In addition to the annotation to specify the action name, add a new annotation to validate the antiforgery token, as shown in Listing 3-15. The antiforgery token is a value that is generated in the server and is passed to the form in the view to be

rendered along with the rest of the fields for the user to enter. This value is brought back with the user-typed values and evaluated to prevent cross-site request forgery attacks. You start the action by validating the information, ensuring that everything is following the security rules. If everything is right, then just call the CreateStudentAsync() method from the repository. If all goes well, it should take the user back to the list of students. If there is an error, the form will stay open, showing any errors to the user.

Listing 3-15. Actions to Create New Student Documents

```
// GET: Student/Create
public ActionResult Create()
{
    return View();
}

// POST: Student/Create
[HttpPost]
[ActionName("Create")]
[ValidateAntiForgeryToken]
public async Task<ActionResult> CreateAsync(Student student)
{
    if (!ModelState.IsValid)
        return View(student);

    try
    {
        await Repository<Student>.CreateStudentAsync(student);
        return RedirectToAction("Index");
    }
```

```
catch
{
    return View(student);
}
}
```

11. Let's now add the view for this action. Right-click anywhere inside the Create() action and select *Add View*. In the Add View window the name should be Create, the template will be Create, and the Model class will be again Student. Leave the rest of the fields with their default values, as shown in Figure 3-39. Then click the Add button.

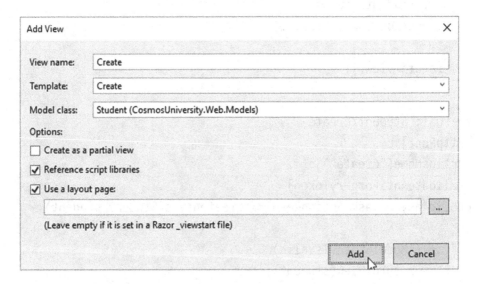

Figure 3-39. Adding the view for the Create action

12. Compile and run the application. Now you have the functionality to create new documents and view the information in them. When you click the Create New link in the students list page, the new form to

create students opens, as shown in Figure 3-40. Type
in some information to create your first document
and you will see something like Figure 3-41.

Figure 3-40. *Form in the Create Student page*

Figure 3-41. *List of students after creating one with your brand new Create Student page*

13. If you click the Details link you should be able to view the information for this particular document. However, as shown in Figure 3-42, an error shows up: *PartitionKey value must be supplied for this operation.* What is happening here is that your collection is partitioned by postal code and Azure Cosmos DB requires the partition key to be able to query the document. In this case, you need to modify the view, controller, and data layer to pass this information.

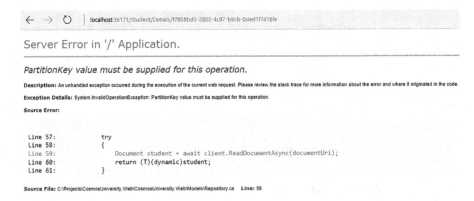

Figure 3-42. *Error when trying to read a document from a partitioned collection without the partition key*

14. Listing 3-16 shows the adjustment needed for the
     Details link in the Index view. Open the Index view
     from the Solution Explorer in the Student folder
     inside the Views folder. This adjustment will be
     needed for all three links to edit, view details, and
     delete documents because they all deal with a single
     document.

Listing 3-16. Adjustments to the Index View to Pass the Partition
Key to Execute the Operations

```
<td>
    @Html.ActionLink("Edit", "Edit",
                    new { id=item.Id, pk = item.PostalCode }) |
    @Html.ActionLink("Details", "Details",
                    new { id=item.Id, pk = item.PostalCode }) |
    @Html.ActionLink("Delete", "Delete",
                    new { id=item.Id, pk = item.PostalCode })
</td>
```

15. Now let's modify the Details action in the controller
     to receive this value in their signature. Listing 3-17
     shows the modified action.

Listing 3-17. Adjustments in the Controller Actions to Receive the
Value of the Partition Key

```
[ActionName("Details")]
public async Task<ActionResult> DetailsAsync(string id, int pk)
{
    var student = await Repository<Student>.GetStudentAsync(id, pk);
    return View(student);
}
```

16. Finally, the data layer class should be adjusted
     to use the partition key. Listing 3-18 shows
     the adjustment. The new parameter is added
     to the method and it is used to create a new
     RequestOptions object.

Listing 3-18. Adjusted Data Layer Method to Query the Database
for a Particular Document

```
public static async Task<T> GetStudentAsync
                                (string id, int partitionKey)
{
    if (string.IsNullOrEmpty(id))
        throw new ApplicationException("No student id specified");

    Uri documentUri = UriFactory.CreateDocumentUri
                                (_dbName, _collectionName, id);
    try
    {
        RequestOptions requestOptions = new RequestOptions {
            PartitionKey = new PartitionKey(partitionKey)
        };
        Document student = await client.ReadDocumentAsync
                                (documentUri, requestOptions);
        return (T)(dynamic)student;
    }
    catch (DocumentClientException ex)
    {
        if (ex.StatusCode == System.Net.HttpStatusCode.NotFound)
            return null;

        throw;
    }
}
```

17. Now, after compiling and running the application,
     you should see a successful result, as shown in
     Figure 3-43.

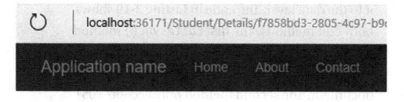

Details

Student

FirstName	John
LastName	Smith
BirthDate	1/1/1989 12:00:00 AM
Address1	123 Main St.
Address2	
City	Chicago
State	IL
PostalCode	60601
PhoneNumber	123-123-1234

Edit | Back to List

Figure 3-43. *Successful query for a single document using a*
partitioned collection

18.   Now you are going to add the code for editing a
      document. In Listing 3-16 you adjusted the link to
      open the Edit page. You need to adjust the action
      in the controller to receive the postal code and pass
      it to the data layer. The code in Listing 3-19 shows
      both Edit methods. The first EditAsync() method
      reads the document from the database and opens
      the page with a form ready to edit the values of the
      document. The second method only accepts POST
      requests, similarly to the CreateAsync() method in
      Listing 3-15. The method also validates the model,
      and if everything looks correct, then it calls the data
      layer using the ReplaceStudentAsync() method.

Listing 3-19. Edit Actions Used to Edit Student Documents

```
// GET: Student/Edit/5
[ActionName("Edit")]
public async Task<ActionResult> EditAsync(string id, int pk)
{
    var student = await Repository<Student>.GetStudentAsync(id, pk);
    return View(student);
}

// POST: Student/Edit/5
[HttpPost]
[ActionName("Edit")]
[ValidateAntiForgeryToken]
public async Task<ActionResult> EditAsync(string id, Student student)
```

```
{
    if (!ModelState.IsValid)
        return View(student);

    try
    {
        await Repository<Student>.ReplaceStudentAsync(student, id);
        return RedirectToAction("Index");
    }
    catch
    {
        return View();
    }
}
```

Note in this case that the partition key was not needed for the actual replace operation; it was needed only to read the document to display the form.

19.   Let's now add the view for the Edit action. Right-click anywhere inside the Edit() action and select *Add View*. In the Add View window the name should be Edit, the template will be Edit, and the Model class will be again Student. Leave the rest of the fields with their default values, as shown in Figure 3-44. Then click the Add button.

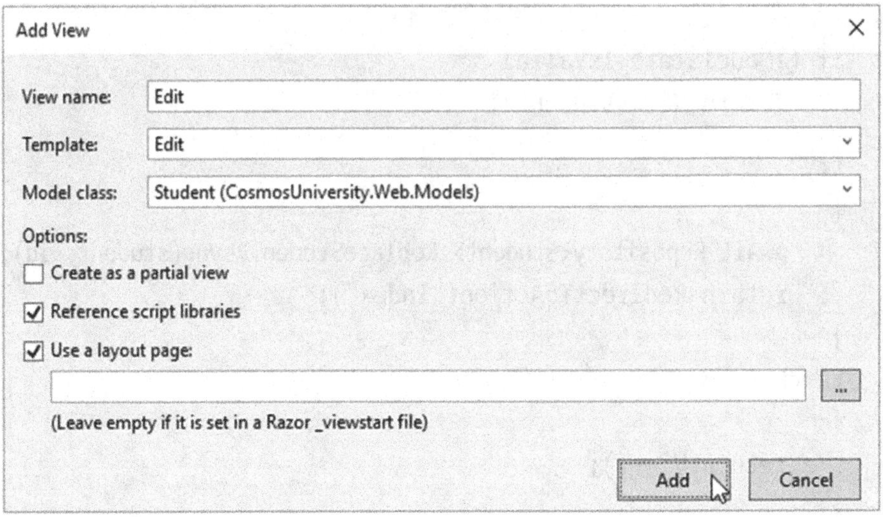

Figure 3-44. The Add View window for the Edit( ) action

20.   Now for the final operation. You are going to add
        the functionality to delete documents. For this you
        are going to adjust the two Delete() actions in the
        controller. First, you'll make them asynchronous, as
        described before. The first action will only render
        the document, similar to the Details() action.
        It will also show a button to perform the actual
        deletion. The second action will accept only POST
        requests and will call DeleteStudentAsync() in the
        data layer. Listing 3-20 shows the complete code.

Listing 3-20. Action Methods to Delete Student Documents

```
// GET: Student/Delete/5
[ActionName("Delete")]
public async Task<ActionResult> Delete(string id, int pk)
```

```
{
    var student = await Repository<Student>.GetStudentAsync(id, pk);
    return View(student);
}

// POST: Student/Delete/5
[HttpPost]
[ActionName("Delete")]
[ValidateAntiForgeryToken]
public async Task<ActionResult> DeleteAsync
                            (string id, int pk, Student student)
{
    try
    {
        await Repository<Student>.DeleteStudentAsync(id, pk);
        return RedirectToAction("Index");
    }
    catch
    {
        return View(student);
    }
}
```

21. In Listing 3-21 you can see the modified code for the
    DeleteStudentAsync() method in the data layer. It
    now handles the partition key that needs to be sent
    in the RequestOptions object.

Listing 3-21. Modified DeleteStudentAsync() Method That Includes
the Partition Key

```
public static async Task<Document> DeleteStudentAsync
                                    (string id, int partitionKey)
{
    if (string.IsNullOrEmpty(id))
        throw new ApplicationException("No student id specified");

    RequestOptions requestOptions = new RequestOptions
    {
        PartitionKey = new PartitionKey(partitionKey)
    };
    Uri documentUri = UriFactory.CreateDocumentUri
                                    (_dbName, _collectionName, id);
    return await client.DeleteDocumentAsync
                                    (documentUri, requestOptions);
}
```

22. Let's now add the view for the Delete action.
     Right-click anywhere inside the Delete() action
     and select *Add View*. In the Add View window
     the name should be Delete, the template will be
     Delete, and the Model class will be again Student.
     Leave the rest of the fields with their default
     values, as shown in Figure 3-45. Then click the
     Add button.

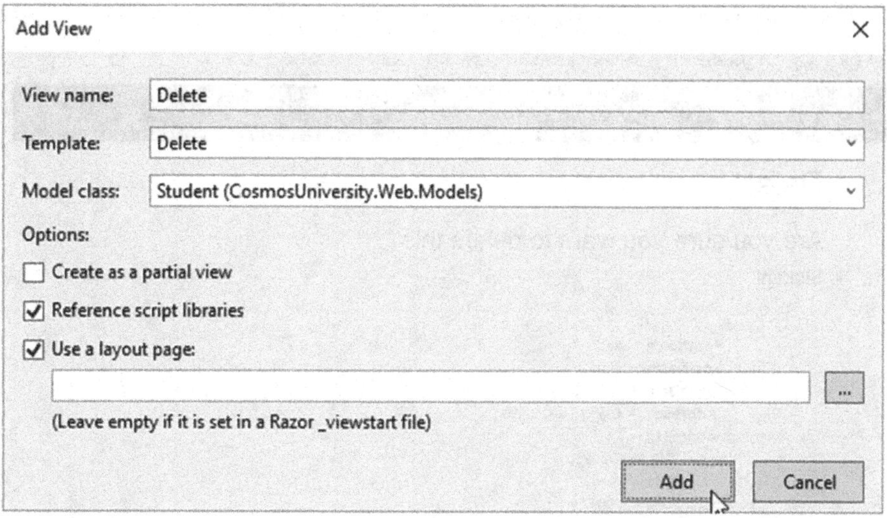

Figure 3-45. *The Add View window for the Delete( ) action method*

When you click the Delete link now, you will see a new page opening up to show the details of the document being deleted and to ask for your confirmation to delete the document (see Figure 3-46). Also note in the URL of the delete page that the id of the document is being passed along with the partition key.

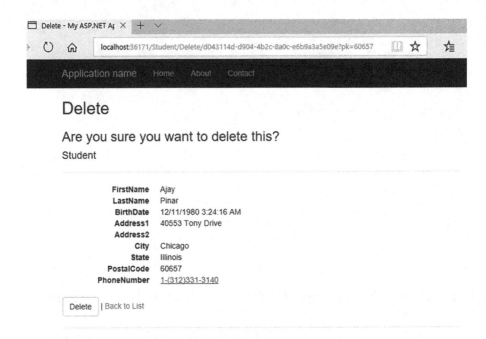

Figure 3-46. *Deleting a document (default scaffold page)*

You now have a full ASP.NET web application that can manipulate documents in an Azure Cosmos DB database with a partitioned collection using the DocumentDB .NET SDK.

Summary

In this chapter, you examined some of the fundamental aspects of working with an Azure Cosmos DB database. You learned how to create a database and collection using the Azure Cosmos DB Emulator. You also learned how to add a partition key to the collection and configure it based on the requirements for your application. Then you examined the basics of creating a document and manipulating documents in the emulator.

The final part of the chapter was devoted to creating a simple ASP.NET web application that implements the DocumentDB .NET SDK to manage documents. You learned the requirements for the web application, such as the necessary packages that need to be downloaded from NuGet Package Manager. You also learned how to create a simple data layer that contains the all the necessary code to interact with an Azure Cosmos DB database, collection, and documents using the DocumentDB .NET SDK.

Along the way you also saw the potential problems when dealing with asynchronous methods and how to resolve them, as well as problems when using partitioned collections.

In the next chapter, you will work with processes and tools to import and export data to and from Azure Cosmos DB.

CHAPTER 4

Importing Data into an Azure Cosmos DB Database

One of the most important aspects for any individual or company with an existing application that wants to use Azure Cosmos DB is how to move their existing data to Azure so they don't lose anything. To solve this problem, there are different options in Azure Cosmos DB depending on the source of the data.

In this chapter, you will examine one of the tools to import and export data to and from Azure Cosmos DB. This tool is free, open source, and can be downloaded and used without restrictions.

Introducing the DocumentDB Data Migration Tool

The DocumentDB Data Migration Tool (DMT) is used to migrate (import) data from different sources into an Azure Cosmos DB database that implements the DocumentDB API. The sources of data can include (but are not limited to) the following:

© José Rolando Guay Paz 2018
J. R. Guay Paz, *Microsoft Azure Cosmos DB Revealed,*
https://doi.org/10.1007/978-1-4842-3351-1_4

- JSON files

- SQL Server

- CSV files

- Azure Table storage

- Azure Cosmos DB collections

- Amazon DynamoDB

- HBase

- MongoDB

The DMT can be obtained in two forms. You can download the most recent version of the executable from Microsoft at `http://bit.ly/cosmos-db-ddbdmt-download` or you can get the source code, which is open source and hosted on GitHub at `http://bit.ly/cosmos-db-ddbdmt-source`.

Tip   If you are a developer, the availability of the DMT's source code gives you a great opportunity to not just look at the internals of the tool but to help make it better by fixing bugs and providing improvements. I encourage you to get involved in open source projects, especially this one.

Software Requirements

The DMT is supported in the following operating systems:

- Windows 10

- Windows 7 Service Pack 1

- Windows 8

- Windows 8.1

- Windows Server 2008 R2 SP1

- Windows Server 2008 Service Pack 2

- Windows Server 2012

- Windows Server 2012 R2

- Windows Vista Service Pack 2

To run or build the DMT, ensure you have .NET Framework 4.5.1 or higher installed.

Features of the DocumentDB Data Migration Tool

While the DMT is a simple tool, it includes a number of features that are important for importing data. The following list includes some of these features:

- **Multiple interfaces**: You can use the DMT in two ways: the graphical user interface (GUI) or the command line interface (CLI). Both versions of the program are included in the download package and source code.

- **Multiple sources**: The DMT supports reading data from multiple files sources such as JSON and CSV files, other NoSQL databases such as MongoDB and Amazon DynamoDB, and relational databases such as SQL Server.

- **CLI command from GUI**: The GUI exposes an option to generate the equivalent CLI command used for the import operation. This is particularly useful to automate import processes and the CLI command is unknown.

- **Available source code**: The source code of the tool is available from GitHub at `http://bit.ly/cosmos-db-ddbdmt-source`.

- **Bulk and sequential imports**: In addition to sequential imports, you can perform bulk imports using an Azure Cosmos DB stored procedure.

Installing the DocumentDB Data Migration Tool

The installation of the DMT is very simple. The following steps will guide you through the process of obtaining the latest version of the executable:

1. To obtain the latest version of the DMT's executable, open your browser and go to `http://bit.ly/cosmos-db-ddbdmt-download`. Figure 4-1 shows the download page.

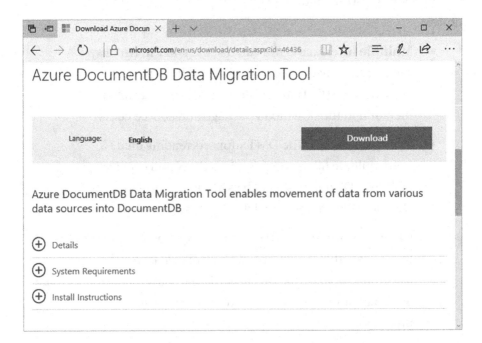

Figure 4-1. Download page for the DocumentDB Data Migration Tool

2. On the download page, click the orange Download button. This action will open the download options shown in Figure 4-2. The two options are a Microsoft Word document with information about how to use the tool and a zip file with the tool files. Check both options and then click the Next button.

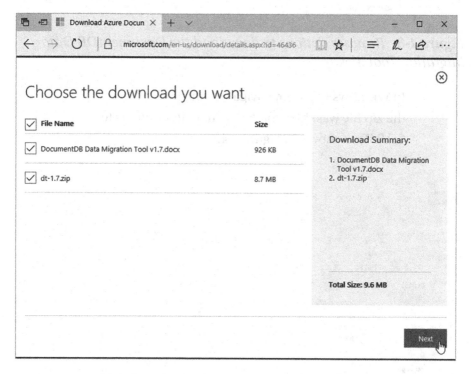

Figure 4-2.   Download options for the DocumentDB Data Migration Tool

3. Depending on your browser and configuration, you will be prompted to open or save the files. In my case, it shows the options in Figure 4-3. Click Save to keep a copy of the files. If prompted, select the folder where you want to save the files.

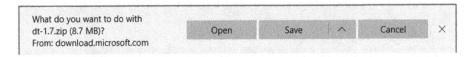

Figure 4-3. *Browser options to download the DocumentDB Data Migration Tool files*

4. In Windows Explorer, navigate to the folder where the zip file was downloaded. Extract its contents to C:\DMT, as shown in Figure 4-4.

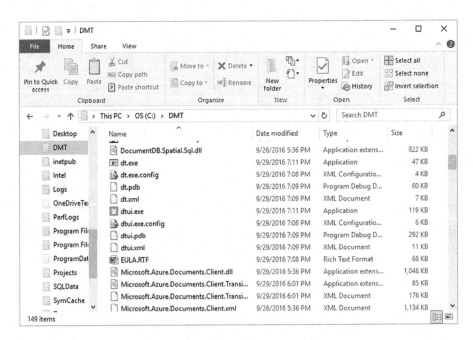

Figure 4-4. *Contents of the zip file in the C:\DMT folder*

5. Double-click the `dtui.exe` file to test the tool. You should see the window shown in Figure 4-5.

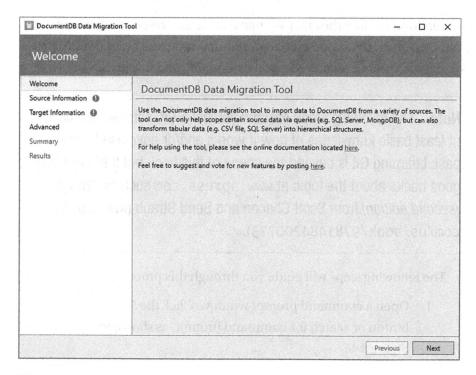

Figure 4-5. *DocumentDB Data Migration Tool graphical interface*

If you see the same window as in Figure 4-5 then you have successfully downloaded and installed the DocumentDB Data Migration Tool.

Installing the DocumentDB Data Migration Tool from the Source Code

As mentioned before the DMT is open source and you can download it from GitHub. Let's now download the source code and build the DMT so you have a working version that you can modify and improve.

Note   The following steps assume you have Git installed and have at least basic knowledge of how it works and/or have used it in the past. Learning Git is beyond the scope of this book but there are very good books about the topic at www.apress.com such as *Pro Git (second edition)* from Scott Chacon and Bend Straub (www.apress.com/us/book/9781484200773).

The following steps will guide you through this process:

1. Open a command prompt window. Click the Start button or search for command prompt, as shown in Figure 4-6.

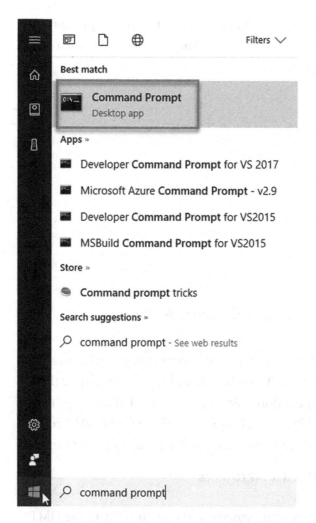

Figure 4-6. *Searching for the Command Prompt desktop app*

2. Click the Command Prompt desktop app icon. This
    will open a window similar to the one shown in
    Figure 4-7.

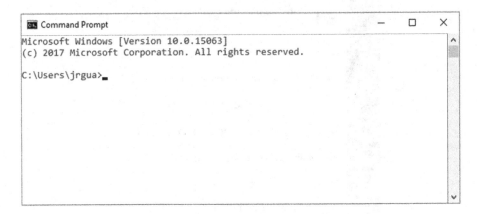

Figure 4-7. *Command Prompt desktop app*

3. When you created the sample application in
    Chapter 3, you had a `Projects` folder where the
    application's files were created. Let's change to the
    `C:\Projects` folder. You will store the DMT source
    code in this folder. Use the following command:

    `C:\>cd C:\Projects`

4. Open your browser and type the URL of the DMT
    source code in GitHub (`http://bit.ly/cosmos-
    db-ddbdmt-source`). When the page opens, click the
    green button to the right of the page that says "Clone
    or download," as shown in Figure 4-8. This will open
    a small window with the two options to clone the
    repository. One is with HTTPS and the second is
    with SSH. Let's use the HTTPS URL for now as it is
    simpler.

Figure 4-8. *Obtaining the repository URL to clone the source code*

5. Click the button to the right of the URL to copy the address to the clipboard. This is illustrated in Figure 4-9. You will need this URL to clone the repository and download the files.

Figure 4-9. *Copying the repository URL to the clipboard*

6. Now go back to the command prompt app and type the command in Listing 4-1. Then press the Enter key. The command will connect to GitHub and download the necessary files from the repository so you can work with it from Visual Studio. It will create a new folder to store the files with the name `azure-documentdb-datamigrationtool` in your `Projects` folder. You should see something like what is shown in Figure 4-10.

Listing 4-1. Cloning the DMT from GitHub

```
C:\Projects>git clone https://github.com/Azure/azure-
documentdb-datamigrationtool.git
```

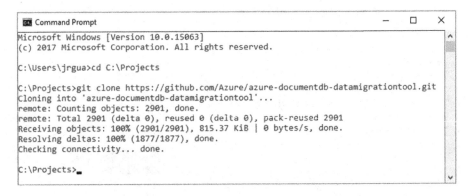

Figure 4-10. *Cloning the DMT repository from GitHub*

7. Open Visual Studio, as shown in Figure 4-11. Click the Start button and scroll to the bottom of the programs to find Visual Studio 2017.

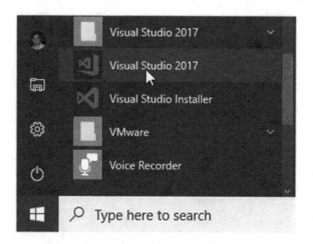

Figure 4-11. *Opening Visual Studio 2017*

8. From Visual Studio, open the DMT solution from the new folder created in step 6. This is shown in Figure 4-12. Note the many folders and files that were downloaded.

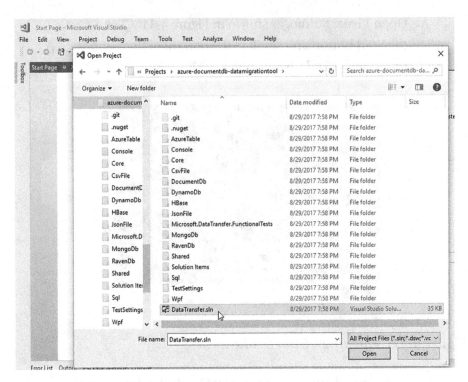

Figure 4-12.   *Opening the DMT source code in Visual Studio*

9.   When the solution opens, you will see many projects
     inside folders in the Solution Explorer window, as
     shown in Figure 4-13. The solution might take a
     while to open.

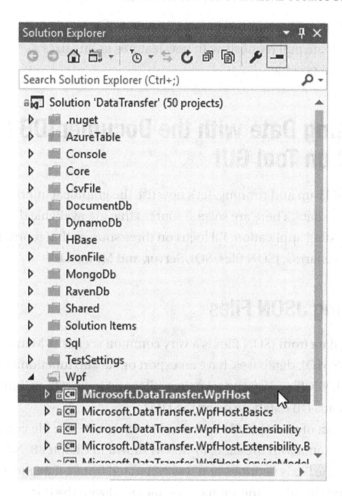

Figure 4-13. *Many projects*

10. As shown in Figure 4-13, open the Wpf folder and
    select the Microsoft.DataTransfer.WpfHost
    project and press F5 to compile the solution and run
    the project. If all goes well, Visual Studio will have
    downloaded all the necessary packages from NuGet,
    compiled the projects, and built the solution. The
    graphical interface application should be running.

From this code, you can troubleshoot any issues and
create pull requests with new features or bug fixes
you provide.

Importing Data with the DocumentDB Data Migration Tool GUI

With the DMT up and running, let's now use the graphical interface to
import some data. There are several sources that are available depending
on your existing application. I'll focus on three sources that represent very
common scenarios: JSON files, SQL Server, and MongoDB.

Importing JSON Files

Importing data from JSON files is a very common scenario. Many systems,
including NoSQL databases, have an export or backup functionality that
generates JSON files. You can take those files and import them into an
Azure Cosmos DB database using the DMT.

An extract of a sample file is shown in Listing 4-2. This file contains
1,000 documents with the same format as shown in Chapter 3. Note that
the data in the file is fictitious and was generated from a data mocking tool.
You can find this file in the source code included with the book.

Listing 4-2. Extract of a JSON File

```
[{"firstName":"Ronda","lastName":"Beecheno","birthDate":"1998-
02-05T14:21:48Z","address1":"57401 Moland Drive","address2":null,
"city":"Harrisburg","state":"Pennsylvania","postalCode":17121,"
phoneNumber":"1-(717)760-6156"},
{"firstName":"Ingelbert","lastName":"Coverdill",
"birthDate":"1988-08-08T11:47:01Z","address1":"09 Lake View
```

```
Drive","address2":null,"city":"Fort Myers","state":"Florida",
"postalCode":33994,"phoneNumber":"1-(239)671-2746"},
{"firstName":"Portia","lastName":"Tuckley","birthDate":
"1991-03-20T06:52:59Z","address1":"081 Coolidge Alley",
"address2":null,"city":"Canton","state":"Ohio",
"postalCode":44720,"phoneNumber":"1-(234)384-0389"},
...
```

Follow the next steps that showcase the usage of the DMT to import a JSON file:

1. Earlier in the chapter you created a folder named DMT in the C: drive in which to save the downloaded zip file that contains the executable version of the DMT. Open the DMT from C:\DMT\dtui.exe. This is shown in Figure 4-14.

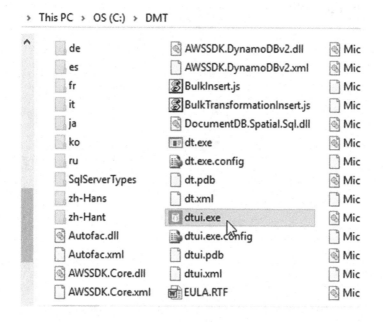

Figure 4-14. Running the DMT graphic interface by launching dtui.exe

2. When you open the DMT graphic interface, you will
    see it is a wizard type program. The first step in the
    wizard is the *Welcome* step. In this step, you will see
    a brief explanation of the tool and some links to get
    more information about it. Click the Next button.

3. You are now in the *Source Information* step. Here is
    where you define the source of the data you want
    to import. From the *Import from* drop-down, select
    JSON file(s). Note in Figure 4-15 that you have four
    options to provide the DMT with a JSON file source.
    You can add a single file, a folder (with an extra
    option to recursively look in inside folders for more
    files), a URL, and a BLOB from Azure. An interesting
    feature of the DMT is that you can add multiple files,
    folders, URLs, or BLOBs and they will be processed
    by the tool.

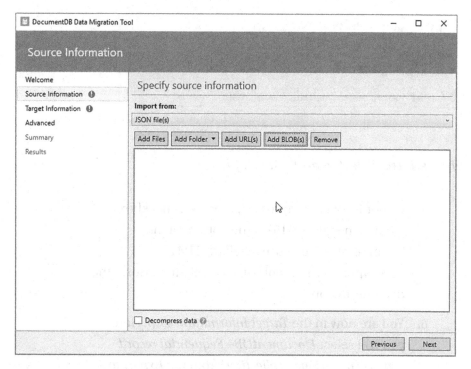

Figure 4-15. *Selecting the source file for the DMT*

4. For now, select a JSON file from the folder where it's stored. It will look something similar to what is shown in Figure 4-16. You can use the sample file in Listing 4-2 from the book's source code or get your own file. Then click the Next button.

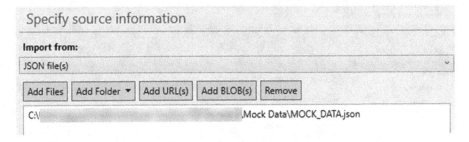

Figure 4-16. *Select to add a JSON file*

5.   If your file was compressed, there is a checkbox
     (shown in Figure 4-15) at the bottom of the
     wizard that you can use to tell the DMT to
     decompress it. The tool will use GZip to perform the
     decompression.

6.   You are now in the *Target Information* step. Here,
     you will select *DocumentDB - Sequential record
     import (partitioned collection)* from the *Export to*
     drop-down, as shown in Figure 4-17.

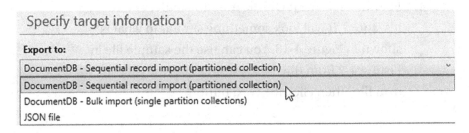

Figure 4-17. *Selecting the destination for the data*

7. Then type the *connection string*. The connection
    string consists of three pieces of information that
    are separated by colons. They are the account
    endpoint, account key, and database. The
    keywords and values used for the connection
    string are shown in Listing 4-3. Once you enter the
    connection string, you can use the Verify button to
    ensure the DMT can connect to your database.

Listing 4-3. Connection String for the Azure Cosmos DB Emulator

```
AccountEndpoint=https://localhost:8081/
AccountKey=
C2y6yDjf5/R+ob0N8A7Cgv30VRDJIWEHLM+4QDU5DE2nQ9nDuVTqobD4b8mGGyP
MbIZnqyMsEcaGQy67XIw/Jw==
Database=cosmosuniversity
```

The full connection string now looks like
```
AccountEndpoint=https://localhost:8081/;AccountKey=
C2y6yDjf5/R+ob0N8A7Cgv30VRDJIWEHLM+4QDU5DE2nQ9nDuVTqobD4b8mGGyP
MbIZnqyMsEcaGQy67XIw/Jw==;Database=cosmosuniversity
```

8. The next step is to enter the name of the collection
    where the documents should be stored. In this
    example, type Student.

9. Then type the key in the collection that is used as the
    partition key. This box is not mandatory, but since
    your collection does have a partition key you need
    to type /postalCode.

10. The next field determines the throughput you want
    for the collection. If the collection doesn't previously
    exist, it will be created and this value will be used for
    the throughput. If it does exist, it will be ignored.

145

11. Finally, the last field is used to know the id field in the documents. In the case of the sample JSON file, there is no id field, so you can leave the file blank. If you do have one in your file, then you need to specify it here to avoid Azure Cosmos DB autogenerating ids for your documents.

12. At this point, the wizard step should look like Figure 4-18. Click the Next button.

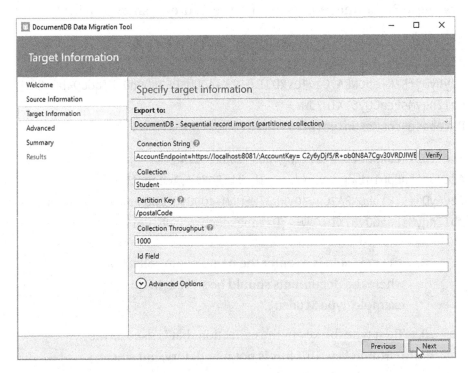

Figure 4-18. *Fields necessary to connect to the Azure Cosmos DB database and collection*

13.   There is a set of advanced options shown in
       Figure 4-19. The *Number of Parallel Requests*
       indicates how many documents will be imported
       simultaneously; the default is 10. While there is no
       limit to this number, you need to pay attention to
       your provisioned throughput because if you hit the
       limit, some documents can fail. *Disable Automatic
       Id Generation* instructs the tool explicitly to not
       generate ids for the documents you are importing.
       This works in conjunction with the id field explained
       earlier because you would need to define the id
       field and any document that doesn't have such id
       won't be imported. *Update Existing Documents* will
       look to see if the document being imported already
       exists based on its id; if so, the document gets
       replaced. *Persists Date and Time as* is a setting that
       indicates if date and time fields should be treated as
       strings, epoch (Unix time), or both. *Indexing policy*
       determines how indexes should be managed; the
       default is blank, which will use the default setting
       in the Azure Cosmos DB database indexing policy.
       You can type the policy settings or you can use a file
       with the settings. The *Number of Retries on Failure*
       indicates how many times the DMT will retry to
       import the documents. *Connection Mode* determines
       how to connect to the database. *DirectTcp* is the
       default but you can use *DirectHttps* or *Gateway*
       depending on the network rules. In this example,
       leave all these options with their default values.

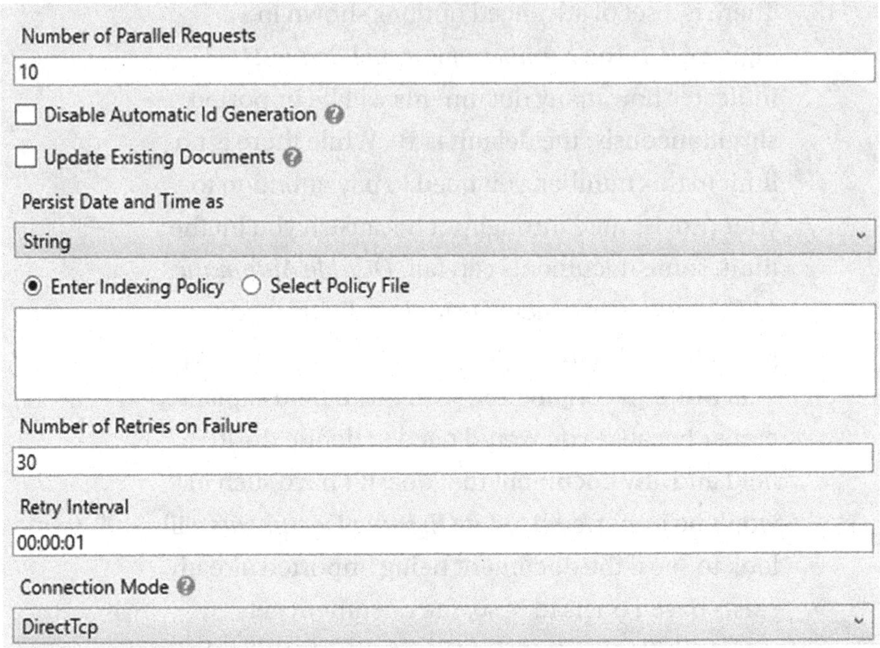

Number of Parallel Requests

10

☐ Disable Automatic Id Generation ❓

☐ Update Existing Documents ❓

Persist Date and Time as

String ⌄

◉ Enter Indexing Policy   ○ Select Policy File

Number of Retries on Failure

30

Retry Interval

00:00:01

Connection Mode ❓

DirectTcp ⌄

Figure 4-19. DocumentDB Data Migration Tool advanced options

14.   Next, in the *Advanced* step, you have the option
      to specify a file for logging all of the information
      generated by the DMT, the level of logging, and the
      interval at which the log should be saved. Figure 4-20
      shows some settings I use when importing data.
      Normally I like to save a log and get as much
      information as possible, so I recommend selecting
      "All" for error information and the interval of 1
      second. Note that for large imports these settings
      might be overwhelming. Now click the Next button.

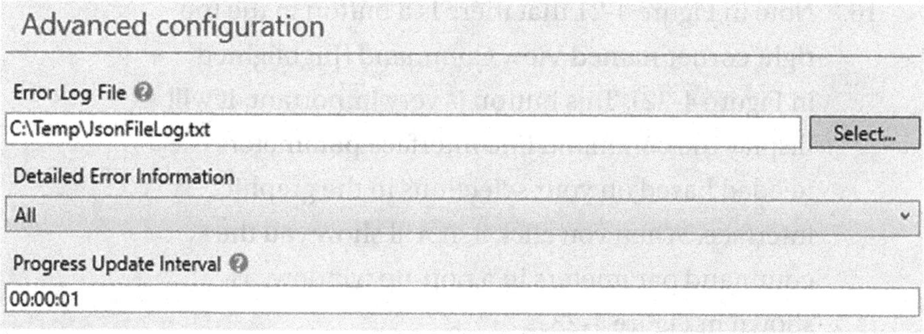

Advanced configuration

Error Log File @

C:\Temp\JsonFileLog.txt

[Select...]

Detailed Error Information

All

Progress Update Interval @

00:00:01

Figure 4-20. *Advanced configuration*

15. The final step is the *Summary* of what the DMT will
do. Here is your last chance to review your selections
and go back to adjust anything that is needed. This is
shown in Figure 4-21.

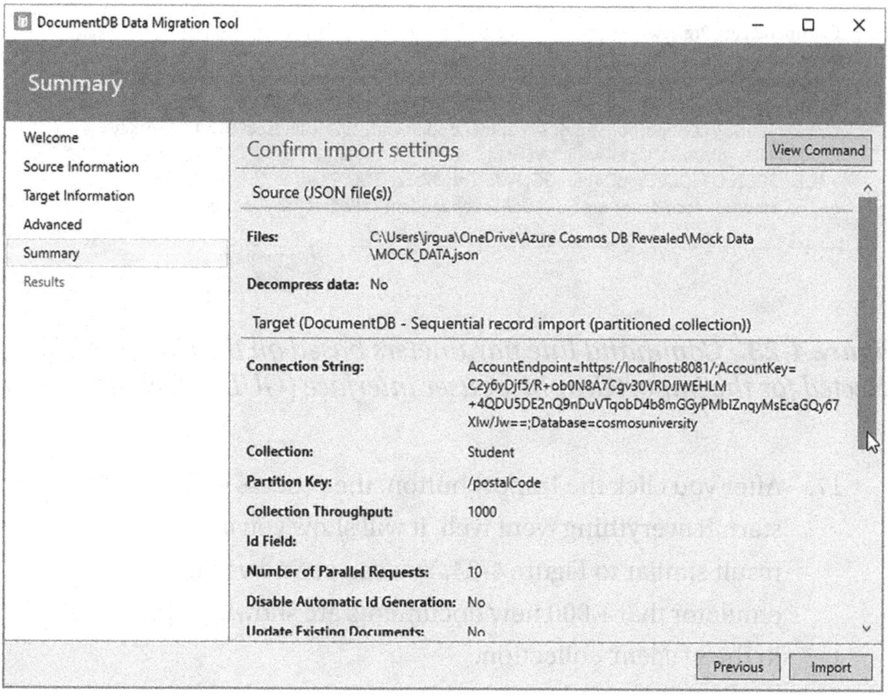

Figure 4-21. *Summary step of the DocumentDB Data Migration Tool*

16.   Note in Figure 4-21 that there is a button in the top
      right corner named View Command (highlighted
      in Figure 4-22). This button is very important. It will
      display the command line interface parameters
      needed based on your selections in the graphic
      interface. When you click it, it will show you the
      command parameters in a pop-up window, as
      shown in Figure 4-23.

Figure 4-22. *View Command button in the Summary step*

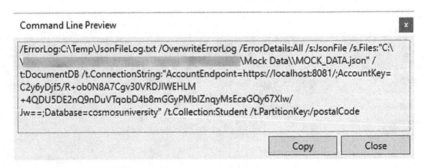

Figure 4-23. *Command line parameters based on the configuration selected for the importGraphical user interface (GUI):JSON files:*

17.   After you click the Import button, the process will
      start. If everything went well, it will show you a
      result similar to Figure 4-24. You can see now in the
      emulator that 1,000 new documents are showing up
      in the student collection.

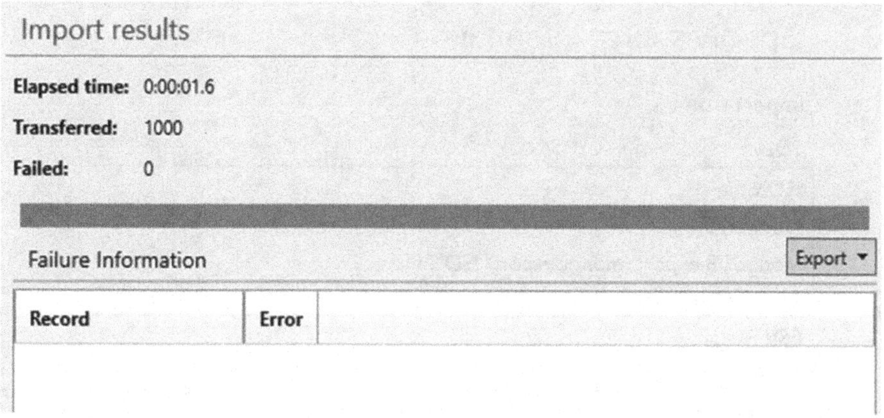

Import results

Elapsed time: 0:00:01.6

Transferred: 1000

Failed: 0

Failure Information   Export ▾

Record	Error	

Figure 4-24. *New documents in the student collection*

Importing from SQL Server

The process to import data from SQL Server is very similar to importing from JSON files. The only difference is in the *Source Information* step. In the following steps, you will learn the differences in importing data from SQL Server to Azure Cosmos DB. Note that this option works perfectly well for on-premises SQL Server or Azure SQL Database.

1. In the *Source Information* step, select *SQL* from the *Import from* drop-down, as shown in Figure 4-25.

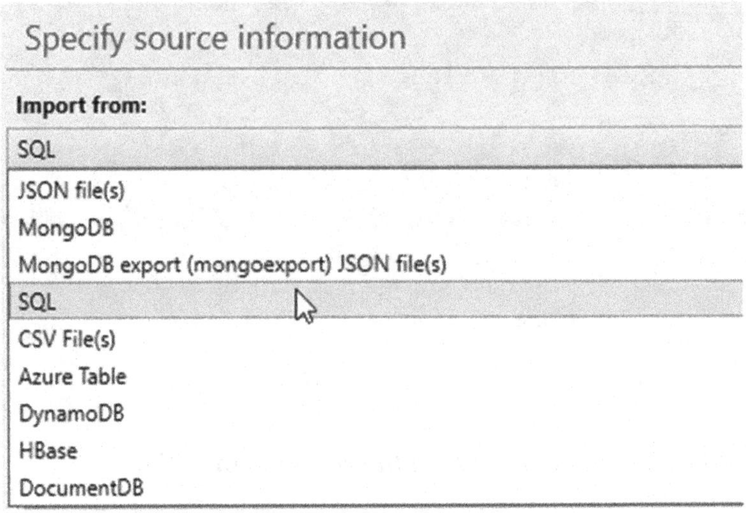

Specify source information

Import from:

SQL
JSON file(s)
MongoDB
MongoDB export (mongoexport) JSON file(s)
SQL
CSV File(s)
Azure Table
DynamoDB
HBase
DocumentDB

Figure 4-25. *Select SQL from the Import from drop-down to import from SQL Server*

2.   The next field is the connection string. This connection string is similar to any other SQL Provider connection string used in .NET applications for the SqlClient library. It is a collection of key-value pairs separated by colon. Listing 4-4 shows two versions of a valid connection string. The first one uses *Windows Authentication* and the second one uses *SQL Server Authentication.* The *Data Source* parameter indicates the server where SQL Server is installed. It can be an IP address or a domain name or the server name and it can also have a port number. *Initial Catalog* defines the name of the database to which you are connecting. *Integrated Security* defines whether Windows Authentication will be used or not. A value of yes or SSPI will configure the connection with

Windows Authentication. *User ID* and *Password* are used when SQL Server Authentication is used for the credentials of the login. *Persists Security Info* determines whether or not to return security-sensitive information such as the password after the connection is open. Setting this parameter to false is strongly recommended. More information about connection strings for SQL Server can be found at http://bit.ly/connection-string. For this sample application, use the connection string format that you have available.

Listing 4-4. Connections Strings with Windows Authentication and SQL Server Authentication

```
// Windows Authentication
Data Source=(local);Initial Catalog=CosmosUniversitySQL;
Integrated Security=SSPI;Persist Security Info=False

// SQL Server Authentication
Data Source=(local);Initial Catalog=CosmosUniversitySQL;
User ID=cosmos;Password=P@ssw0rd;Persist Security Info=False
```

3. The last piece information that is required is the query or file with the query to use to read the data from SQL Server. For this example, let's read all the columns and records in the Student table, as shown in Figure 4-26.

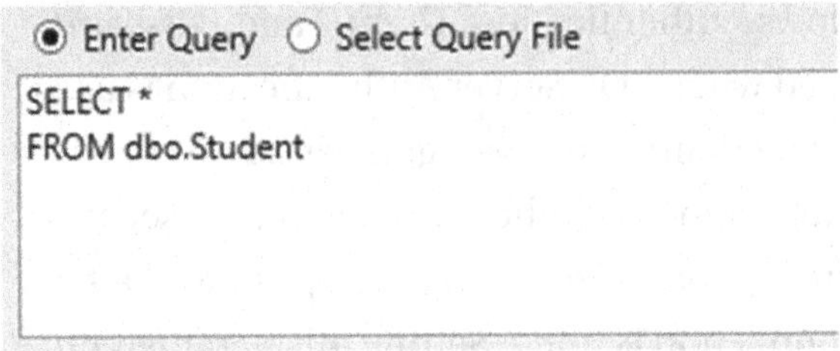

Figure 4-26. Query to use to read the data that will be imported into Azure Cosmos DB

4. If your query will be used to manage complex documents, you can use the additional field at the bottom of the step screen named *Nesting Separator*. This field is used to enter the delimiter to split columns names into subdocuments.

5. At this point, everything is ready and you can click the Next button. You can then follow the instructions from the "Importing JSON Files" section, starting on step 6 to complete the import operation.

Importing from MongoDB

When importing documents from a MongoDB database, all the differences in the DMT happen in the *Source Information* step. This is similar to when importing from SQL Server. The following steps describe what is needed:

1. In the *Source Information* step, select *MongoDB* from the *Import from* drop-down, as shown in Figure 4-27.

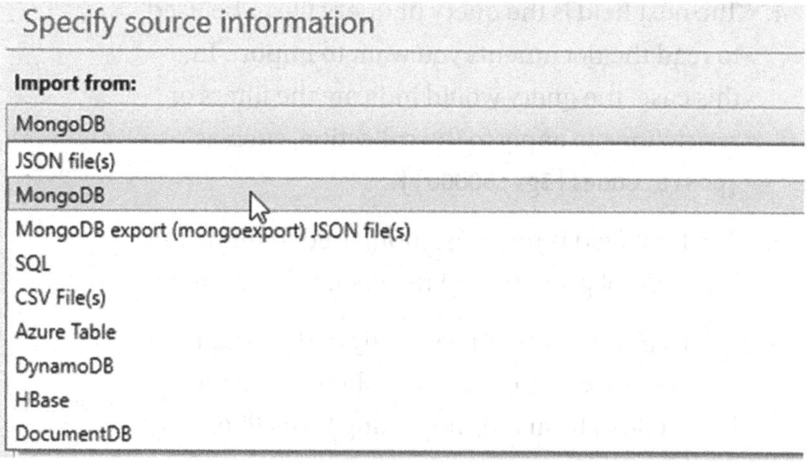

Specify source information

Import from:

| MongoDB |
| JSON file(s) |
| MongoDB |
| MongoDB export (mongoexport) JSON file(s) |
| SQL |
| CSV File(s) |
| Azure Table |
| DynamoDB |
| HBase |
| DocumentDB |

Figure 4-27. *Select MongoDB from the Import from drop-down to import documents from a MongoDB database*

2. The next field is the connection string to connect to your MongoDB database. The connection string format is different than the one from SQL Server. Listing 4-5 shows the format of the connection string for a MongoDB database. You need to know the username and password of a user with at least read permissions for the database and collection. Then you need the server and port for the database as well as the name of the database.

Listing 4-5. MongoDB Connection String Format

```
mongodb://<dbuser>:<dbpassword>@<server>:<port>/<database>
```

3. Next you need to enter the collection you want to read documents from.

4. The next field is the query or query file to be used
    to read the documents you want to import. In
    this case, the query would indicate the filters or
    restrictions to apply to the collection, such as
    {postalCode:{$gt:60000}}.

5. The final field is the projection, used to refine the
    selection of properties in the document to import.

6. At this point, everything is ready and you can
    click the Next button. You can then follow the
    instructions from the "Importing JSON Files"
    section, starting on step 6 to complete the import
    operation.

Importing Data with the DocumentDB Data Migration Tool Command Line Interface

Using the command line interface of the DMT is done by running the
program dt.exe and passing the necessary parameters.

As an example, see Listing 4-6, which runs the dt.exe program from
the C:\DMT folder you created earlier. This example uses the parameters
generated for the JSON files import in the "Importing JSON Files" section
that is shown in Figure 4-23.

Listing 4-6. Command to Import Data with the CLI

```
C:\DMT\dt.exe /ErrorLog:C:\Temp\JsonFileLog.txt
/OverwriteErrorLog /ErrorDetails:All /s:JsonFile
/s.Files:"C:\\Mock Data\\MOCK_DATA.json" /t:DocumentDB
/t.ConnectionString:"AccountEndpoint=https://localhost:8081/;
AccountKey= C2y6yDjf5/R+ob0N8A7Cgv30VRDJIWEHLM+4QDU5DE2nQ9nDuVT
qobD4b8mGGyPMbIZnqyMsEcaGQy67XIw/Jw==;Database=cosmosuniversity"
/t.Collection:student /t.PartitionKey:/postalCode
```

This functionality is particularly important to automate imports that need to happen either on a schedule or as part of a DevOps strategy.

If you run this command, you will see the DMT working as shown in Figure 4-28.

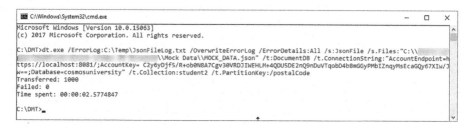

Figure 4-28. *Importing data with the CLI*

Summary

In this chapter, you worked with the DocumentDB Data Migration Tool. In the first part, you learned about the tool, its requirements, features, and benefits. Then you saw how to obtain the tool from two different sources. One was using the executable version that is ready to use, the second was with the source code from GitHub. With the second approach, you have the ability to learn how the tool is built and to contribute to its development.

In the second part of the chapter you learned how to import data into an Azure Cosmos DB database, first from JSON files, then from SQL Server, and lastly from a MongoDB database. The process is quite simple using the GUI, which also provides a mechanism to generate the necessary information to run the CLI. At the end of the chapter you saw how to use the parameters generated from the GUI to automate the import process with the CLI.

In the following chapter, you will examine indexing and querying in more detail.

CHAPTER 5

Querying an Azure Cosmos DB Database

An integral part of working with any database is the ability to query the data in the database. Fortunately, this very important functionality has been implemented in Azure Cosmos DB in a way that any previous SQL experience is valid and will help you accomplish even the most complex tasks.

A related topic to querying is indexing. Let's review the indexing policies in Azure Cosmos DB, how they work, and how they can be modified to achieve better throughput.

Understanding Indexing

In Azure Cosmos DB, as opposed to relational database systems, every document is indexed by default. That means that in any collection, documents have indexes in all the properties in the document. This normally works very well for the majority of applications; however, there are times when a different indexing policy might achieve better results.

© José Rolando Guay Paz 2018
J. R. Guay Paz, *Microsoft Azure Cosmos DB Revealed,*
https://doi.org/10.1007/978-1-4842-3351-1_5

Every collection in a database has a default index policy which is defined by the following properties:

1. The index mode is *consistent.*

2. Documents are indexed *automatically.*

3. All properties are indexed.

Listing 5-1 shows the default index policy for a collection in a database that implements the DocumentDB API.

Listing 5-1. Default Index Policy

```
{
  "indexingMode": "consistent",
  "automatic": true,
  "includedPaths": [
    {
      "path": "/*",
      "indexes": [
        {
          "kind": "Range",
          "dataType": "Number",
          "precision": -1
        },
        {
          "kind": "Range",
          "dataType": "String",
          "precision": -1
        },
```

```
    {
      "kind": "Spatial",
      "dataType": "Point"
    }
  ]
  }
],
"excludedPaths": []
}
```

In the default index policy, you can see the properties described before. The indexing mode is set to consistent, defined by the indexingMode property. The documents are indexed automatically, which is defined by the automatic property being set to true. The includedPaths define which properties in the documents are indexed. By having a value of /* in the path property and by having an empty excludedPaths list, the policy states that all properties should be indexed.

Note   The indexing policy can only be changed in the Azure portal. This functionality is not available in the Azure Cosmos DB Emulator.

To find the index policy, just open the database in the Azure portal, scroll down to *Collection Settings*, select the *collection* from the drop-down, and click the *Default* index policy, as shown in Figure 5-1.

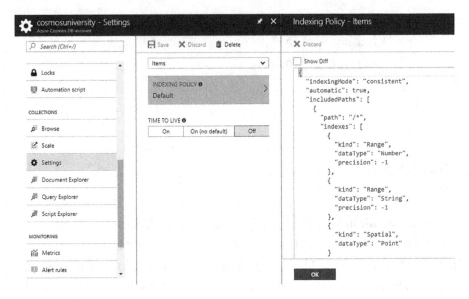

Figure 5-1. *Collection default index policy*

Understanding the Indexing Mode

The indexing mode determines *when* indexes are updated. Azure Cosmos DB provides three different indexing modes:

- **Consistent**: With a *consistent* indexing mode, indexes are updated synchronously as part of the write operation (create, replace, or delete). This might have an impact on write throughput depending on how many properties the document has and the number of writes that happen in a given period of time. Queries follow the same consistency mode as the database (i.e. strong, bounded-staleness, session, consistent prefix, or eventual). This mode is generally acceptable for most workloads.

- **Lazy**: For scenarios where there is a huge amount of data to be ingested into a collection, you can use *lazy* indexing. This mode will change the way indexes are updated from synchronous to asynchronous, causing queries to achieve eventual consistency. This mode is for extremely fast writes where reads are not needed immediately. In addition, lazy mode consumes less RUs than consistent mode.

- **None**: When you select *None* as the indexing mode, you are effectively telling Azure Cosmos DB to not index the documents in the collection. If indexes were previously created as part of a different indexing mode, the change to *None* will drop such indexes, leaving the documents in the collection accessible only to be queried by the *Id* or by reading a document with the *self-URL*. This indexing mode can be useful if your collection is a key-value storage and documents are accessed only by their Id property.

Understanding Index Paths

In an Azure Cosmos DB database, JSON documents are treated like trees, and their properties are mapped as paths in the tree hierarchy. A path starts at the root of the document denoted with / and typically ends with ?. The ? operator indicates that there are multiple values for the specified property.

Take for example the document in Listing 5-2. The path to read the last name property is /lastName. The path to read the age of a children is /children/age/?. And the path to read one of the classes is /children/school/classes[0]/name/?.

Other patterns for paths are * and [ ]. The * pattern indicates everything after such property. For example, the path /children/school/* is referencing all properties under the school property (i.e. grade and

classes). The [ ] pattern indicates all elements in an array. For example,
/children/school/[ ]/name? references name properties in the classes
array under the school property.

Listing 5-2. Sample JSON Document

```
{
        "firstName": "Jose",
        "lastName": "Guay",
        "children":[
                {
                        "name": "Sara",
                        "age": "16",
                        "school":{
                                "grade": "11",
                                "classes":[
                                        {
                                            "name": "Pre-Calculus"
                                        },
                                        {
                                            "name": "US History"
                                        },
                                        {
                                            "name": "Physics"
                                        }
                                ]
                        }
                },
                {
                        "name": "Samantha",
                        "age": "7",
```

```
"school":{
        "grade": "2",
        "classes":[
                {
                    "name": "Math"
                },
                {
                    "name": "Reading"
                },
                {
                    "name": "Music"
                }
            ]
        }
    ]
}
```

Adjusting the Indexing Policy

The indexing policy can be set for specific paths and there are several properties that you can modify to fit the needs of your application. The properties are kind, data type, and precision.

- **Kind** determines the type of index to be applied. It can be *hash*, *range*, or *spatial*. A hash index is best suited for equality comparisons which are used in joins and where clauses. A range index is efficient for equality, range queries (using the operators >, >=, <, <= or !=), and for sorting with the order-by clause. Spatial indexes are designed for queries involving spatial properties like points, polygons, and lines.

- **dataType** identifies the type of data in a path. It can be *number, string, point, polygon,* or *LineString.* An important consideration is that in each path in the indexing policy the different values for the data type can only be defined once. For example, in Listing 5-2, the indexing policy for the path /lastName would include only one definition for the data type *number* and one for *string,* but you can't define *string* a second time.

- **Precision** determines the amount of data an index stores based on how exact comparisons need to be. For hash indexes, the value is any integer between 1 and 8, with 3 as the default. For a range index, the value can be -1 (the default), which indicates maximum precision, and then any value between 1 and 100 (100 also indicates maximum precision). When using the maximum precision for numbers, each value is stored in 8 bytes because JSON stores numbers in 8 bytes. Any precision that is lower than maximum consume less index storage, but in contrast it also causes queries to process more documents, which would potentially consume more RUs.

There are some considerations regarding indexes that you must be aware of:

- If your query uses a range operator but there is no range index for the path, then an error is thrown. This same rule applies for spatial queries and missing spatial indexes.

- If your query has an order-by clause by a path that doesn't have a range index, then an error is thrown.

- If your query has an order-by clause by string properties, you need to define the index precision to maximum (–1).

- Range queries can be performed without a range index using the `x-ms-documentdb-enable-scan` header in the REST API or the `EnableScanInQuery` request option using the .NET SDK.

Querying an Azure Cosmos DB Database

Using the DocumentDB .NET SDK it is very easy to query an Azure Cosmos DB database. There are three syntaxes to query a database: LINQ, Lambda, and SQL. They all do exactly the same work; the only difference is how the queries are written.

Learning the SELECT Statement

To query a database, you need to use the SELECT statement. This statement was first defined in the SQL language, which is the standard for performing operations against a database. Every database product uses SQL in one form or another but they all normally implement one of the standards such as ANSI or ISO and build on top of it its unique features.

If you are familiar with the SELECT statement, you can skip this section because it explains the statement syntax.

As explained earlier, every database implements its own version of SQL and therefore the features for each statement. Because of this, I will only explain the most basic syntax, which you can find generally implemented in most database products.

For the SELECT statement to return any information you need to define at least two pieces of information. The first one is where the data is stored; this is normally tables in the case of relational databases or collections in the case of NoSQL databases. The second piece is the columns (in the case of relational databases) or properties (in the case of NoSQL databases) from the data store.

To achieve its purpose, the SELECT statement is defined by two mandatory clauses: SELECT to define the columns or properties, and FROM to indicate where the data is. The minimal required syntax for the SELECT statement is shown in Listing 5-3.

Listing 5-3. Minimal Syntax for the SELECT Statement

```
SELECT [columns or properties]
FROM [table or collection]
```

In addition to these two clauses, there are two more that are important. Since databases can store a lot of information, you normally try to get what is relevant to you. To solve this, there is a clause that can filter the results you want. This clause is called WHERE. With WHERE, you define the filters to apply to selectively get the relevant information. Finally, results can be sorted when they are returned. To specify the sort order, you use the ORDER BY clause. You use this clause to define the columns or properties that should be used to sort the results and the direction (ascending or descending) for each of them. Listing 5-4 shows the general syntax with these two additional clauses. Remember that you can find these four clauses for the SELECT statement in virtually any database, but each database implements more features and you should read the documentation to find what's available and unique about the database you are using.

Listing 5-4. Extended Syntax of the SELECT Statement

```
SELECT [columns or properties]
FROM [table or collection]
WHERE [filters]
ORDER BY [sort order]
```

Understanding the SELECT Clause

The SELECT clause lets you define the properties or values you want to read from a collection. In addition to specifying the list of properties, you can use the special operator * that indicates *all properties*.

Listing 5-5 shows the usage of the * operator. This tells Cosmos DB to read all properties from the Person collection. For example, in Listing 5-2, the document refers to a collection called Person.

Listing 5-5. Querying All Properties from a Collection

```
SELECT *
FROM Person
```

The result of executing the query in Listing 5-5 is the entire document, as shown in Listing 5-2. If you only need to read a subset of properties, you can just create a list of the properties separated by commas, as shown in Listing 5-6.

Listing 5-6. Querying a Subset of Properties from a Collection

```
SELECT firstName, lastName
FROM Person
```

The result of the query in Listing 5-6 is

```
[{
        "firstName": "Jose",
        "lastName": "Guay"
}]
```

You can also modify the name of the properties with an alias. An alias is a name that you specify with the keyword AS. In Listing 5-7, the query returns the same two columns as in Listing 5-6 but the difference is that the properties will have a different name.

Listing 5-7. Query with Property Aliases

```
SELECT firstName AS "First Name", lastName AS "Last Name"
FROM Person
```

The results of the query from Listing 5-7 are

```
[{
        "First Name": "Jose",
        "Last Name": "Guay"
}]
```

The SELECT clause also supports JSON expressions, as shown in Listing 5-8.

Listing 5-8. Query with JSON Expression

```
SELECT {"First Name": firstName, "Last Name": lastName}
FROM Person
```

In this case, the results are

```
[{
        "$1": {
                "First Name": "Jose",
                "Last Name": "Guay"
        }
}]
```

In this case, what is happening is that the SELECT clause is creating a JSON object, but since there is no key provided, an implicit argument named $1 is automatically created. The implicit arguments are named $1, $2, and so forth. If, on the other hand, a key is defined, as shown in Listing 5-9, then the result is a little different.

Listing 5-9. Query with JSON Expression

```
SELECT {"First": firstName, "Last": lastName} AS "Name"
FROM Person
```

In this case, the results are

```
[{

    "Name": {
        "First": "Jose",
        "Last": "Guay"
    }
}]
```

The SELECT clause also supports scalar expressions. These expressions can be constants, arithmetic expressions, logical expressions, etc. Listing 5-10 shows some scalar expressions.

Listing 5-10. Query with Scalar Expressions

```
SELECT "This is a simple string",
       1+4/2
```

The results are

```
[

    "$1": "This is a simple string",
    "$2": 3
]
```

Understanding the FROM Clause

In Azure Cosmos DB, the FROM clause indicates the collection from which to read data. While that is the general idea, a particular implementation that you can use instead of the collection is a *subdocument*. A subdocument is nothing more than a part of the whole document in the collection. For example, in Listing 5-2, the document contains a subdocument named `Person.children`.

In Listing 5-11, the query retrieves all properties from a subdocument. The query in Listing 5-5 will return the entire document, while the query in Listing 5-11 will return only the portion in the children array.

Listing 5-11. Querying a Subdocument

```
SELECT *
FROM Person.children
```

For the query in Listing 5-11, the results are

```
":[{
        "name": "Sara",
        "age": "16",
        "school":{
                "grade": "11",
                "classes":[{
                                "name": "Pre-Calculus"
                        },
                        {
                                "name": "US History"
                        },
                        {
                                "name": "Physics"
                        }
                ]
        }
},
```

```
{
        "name": "Samantha",
        "age": "7",
        "school":{
                "grade": "2",
                "classes":[{
                                "name": "Math"
                        },
                        {
                                "name": "Reading"
                        },
                        {
                                "name": "Music"
                        }
                ]
        }
}]
```

A few characteristics of the FROM clause are the following:

- The collections or subdocuments can be aliased. That means that you can assign an alias to the collection or subdocument to reference properties easier. This comes in handy when reading from multiple collections and/or subdocuments (which you will see later in this chapter).

- Once you assign an alias, the original source cannot be found.

- All properties that need to be referenced must be fully qualified to avoid ambiguous bindings.

Listing 5-12 shows the same query in Listing 5-5, but with an alias and only selecting two properties. The alias is defined after the collection name as p. The properties are now fully qualified.

Listing 5-12. Modified Query Using an Alias

```
SELECT p.firstName, p.lastName
FROM Person AS p
```

The results of the query in Listing 5-12 are

```
[{
        "firstName": "Jose",
        "lastName": "Guay"
}]
```

Understanding the WHERE Clause

The WHERE clause is optional and defines the conditions that documents must meet to be included in the results of the query. All conditions specified in the WHERE clause must evaluate to true for a document to be included in the result.

Listing 5-13 shows an example of a query with a condition. In this example, the condition defines that all documents with the value of Guay in the property lastName should be returned.

Listing 5-13. Query with a Simple Condition

```
SELECT p.firstName, p.lastName
FROM Person AS p
WHERE p.lastName = "Guay"
```

The results for this query are

```
[{
        "firstName": "Jose",
        "lastName": "Guay"
}]
```

There are many more operators that can be used in conditions in the WHERE clause, as shown in Table 5-1. These operators can be used to perform different types of comparisons.

Table 5-1. *Operators*

Type of Operator	Operators
Arithmetic	+,-,*,/,%
Bitwise	|, &, ^, <<, >>, >>> (zero-fill right shift)
Logical	AND, OR, NOT
Comparison	=, !=, <, >, <=, >=, <>
String	|| (concatenate)

Listing 5-14 shows how to use an arithmetic operator in one of the conditions.

Listing 5-14. Query with an Arithmetic Operator

```
SELECT name
FROM Person.children
WHERE age > 5
```

The result of this query is

```
[{
        "name": "Sara"
},
{
        "name": "Samantha"
}]
```

The keyword BETWEEN can also be used in the same way as in ANSI/ SQL. It will return documents where the values in the condition fall in the range specified, as shown in Listing 5-15.

Listing 5-15. Using the BETWEEN Keyword

```
SELECT name
FROM Person.children
WHERE age BETWEEN 5 AND 10
```

The results of this query are similar to the previous one for Listing 5-14.

Understanding the ORDER BY Clause

The ORDER BY clause is optional and can be included in queries to specify the order in which to return the results. The clause expects a list of properties separated by commas. Each property can contain an optional argument to identify the direction of the sort. The argument can be either ASC or DESC, for ascending (the default, if nothing is specified) and descending.

The example in Listing 5-16 shows the usage of the ORDER BY clause. The query selects the names of the children subdocument and will return the results ordered by the name in alphabetic order.

Listing 5-16. Using the ORDER BY Clause in a Query

```
SELECT name
FROM Person.children
ORDER BY name ASC
```

The results of the query are

```
[{
        "name": "Samantha"
},
{
        "name": "Sara"
}]
```

Working with Iterations

Azure Cosmos DB implements a way to iterate through arrays in JSON documents by extending the FROM clause. The result of this implementation is a single array with the results of multiple documents. For example, in Listing 5-17 you see a query that returns the names of the children in the Person collection. Note how when having multiple documents, the results are grouped by children in each document. This effect can be seen in the results by the nesting of elements inside brackets ([ ]).

Listing 5-17. Querying the Person.children Subdocument

```
SELECT name
FROM Person.children
```

The results of the query are

```
[
        [{
                "name": "Sara"
        },
```

```
    {
            "name": "Samantha"
    }],
    [{
            "name": "Michael"
    },
    {
            "name": "James"
    }],
    [{
            "name": "Daniel"
    }]
]
```

You can iterate over the JSON documents with the addition of the IN keyword as part of the definition of the source of data. In this example, by changing the FROM clause to use iterations, the result is a single array with all the results, shown in Listing 5-18.

Listing 5-18. Using Iterations

```
SELECT p.name
FROM p IN Person.children
```

The results of the query are

```
[
    {
            "name": "Sara"
    },
    {
            "name": "Samantha"
    },
```

```
    {
            "name": "Michael"
    },
    {
            "name": "James"
    },
    {
            "name": "Daniel"
    }
]
```

Understanding Joins

In relational databases, joins play a key role in reading data from tables where data redundancy has been eliminated (normalized). This feature allows developers to keep a single version of a piece of data and use it across the entire application.

Contrary to relational databases where normalized data is fundamental, NoSQL databases such as Azure Cosmos DB rely on the feature that documents will have no specific schema, which in turn expects a document to include every piece of data required to express the entity it represents. This causes some information to be included (repeated) on each document. For example, in a JSON document representing sales orders, the list of products will include the product name, price, and other necessary properties on each of the documents in the collection.

This particular distinction makes joins function a bit different, although in the end, the concept is similar to those in relational databases. They are similar in the sense that different sources of data will be joined to return a particular set of results; however, they are different in the fact that in NoSQL databases you are joining parts of the document as opposed to joining collections (which are the equivalent of tables).

Consider the query in Listing 5-19. Note that the query is doing a join between the Person collection and the children subdocument. You don't need to specify the keys the join will use because children is a subdocument already, a (possible) part of each person.

Listing 5-19. Query with JOINs

```
SELECT p.lastName as Parent,
       c.name AS Child
FROM Person p
JOIN c IN p.children
```

The results are

```
[
        {
                "Parent": "Guay",
                "Child": "Sara"
        },
        {
                "Parent": "Guay",
                "Child": "Samantha"
        }
]
```

Working with Parameterized SQL Queries

Azure Cosmos DB supports parameterized queries. By implementing parameters, your queries become more robust when handling user input and can prevent traditional SQL injection attacks.

The way this is implemented is with the @ notation which is widely used in SQL Server. The query in Listing 5-20 implements parameters in the WHERE clause.

Listing 5-20. Using Parameterized SQL Queries

```
SELECT *
FROM c IN Person.children
WHERE c.age = @age
```

Using Built-In Functions

Azure Cosmos DB has a number of built-in functions that you can use in your queries. These functions can be categorized as *mathematical functions, type-checking functions, string functions, array functions*, and *spatial functions*. Table 5-2 lists the currently implemented built-in functions (taken from `http://bit.ly/cosmos-db-builtin-functions`).

Table 5-2. *Built-In Functions in Azure Cosmos DB*

Function Group	Operations
Mathematical Functions	ABS, CEILING, EXP, FLOOR, LOG, LOG10, POWER, ROUND, SIGN, SQRT, SQUARE, TRUNC, ACOS, ASIN, ATAN, ATN2, COS, COT, DEGREES, PI, RADIANS, SIN, and TAN
Type-Checking Functions	IS_ARRAY, IS_BOOL, IS_NULL, IS_NUMBER, IS_OBJECT, IS_STRING, IS_DEFINED, and IS_PRIMITIVE
String Functions	CONCAT, CONTAINS, ENDSWITH, INDEX_OF, LEFT, LENGTH, LOWER, LTRIM, REPLACE, REPLICATE, REVERSE, RIGHT, RTRIM, STARTSWITH, SUBSTRING, and UPPER
Array Functions	ARRAY_CONCAT, ARRAY_CONTAINS, ARRAY_LENGTH, and ARRAY_SLICE
Spatial Functions	ST_DISTANCE, ST_WITHIN, ST_INTERSECTS, ST_ISVALID, and ST_ISVALIDDETAILED

The built-in functions can be used in your queries in the same way you would, for example, in SQL Server. See Listing 5-21 for an example of a query that uses some of these functions.

Listing 5-21. Using Built-In Functions in a Query

```
SELECT lastName,
       COUNT(children)
FROM Person
```

The results are

```
[{
        "lastName":"Guay",
        "$1":2
}]
```

Extending the Sample Application

In this chapter, you have learned how to query an Azure Cosmos DB database. Let's examine the sample application, Cosmos University, to add some querying functionality that a potential user would need.

The modifications are as follows:

- Add a drop-down to select a property that will be used for filtering.

- Add a text box to enter a value for the property.

- Add a button to filter the results.

- Add a second drop-down with properties to sort the results.

- Add a third drop-down with the sort direction options (ascending or descending).

The sample application implements Lambda queries but in addition to this, I will also include code using the other syntaxes for querying (LINQ and SQL).

The following steps will guide you through the process:

1. Open Visual Studio 2017 from the Start menu, as shown in Figure 5-2.

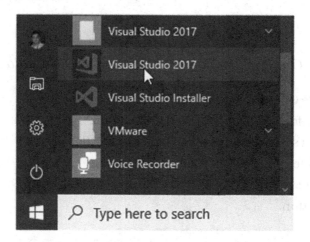

Figure 5-2. *Open Visual Studio 2017 from the Start menu*

2. Go to the *File* menu, select *Open* and from the menu select *Project/Solution*. As shown in Figure 5-3, you can also use the keyboard shortcut of Ctrl-Shift-O.

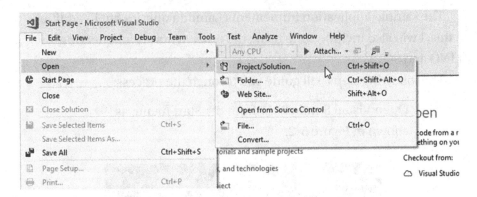

Figure 5-3. *Opening a project or solution in Visual Studio 2017*

3. The Open Project window is open now. Navigate to the folder where you saved the solution. In Chapter 3, you saved it in the C:\Projects\CosmosUniversity folder. As shown in Figure 5-4, select the CosmosUniversity.Web.sln file and click the Open button.

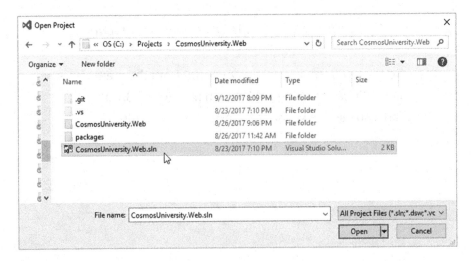

Figure 5-4. *Opening the CosmosUniversity.Web.sln solution*

4. Open the `Index.cshtml` view from the `Views/`
    `Student` folder, as shown in Figure 5-5. This is where
    you will add the drop-downs, text box, and button.

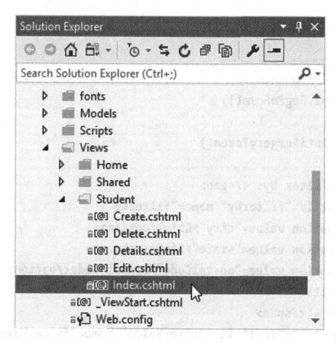

Figure 5-5. *Opening the Index.cshtml view from the Views/Student folder*

5. Add the new HTML markup for the controls, as
    shown in Listing 5-22. This code will create the
    drop-downs, text box, and button that you need to
    implement the filtering and sorting.

Listing 5-22. New HTML Markup for the Controls

```
@model IEnumerable<CosmosUniversity.Web.Models.Student>

@{
    ViewBag.Title = "Index";
}

<h2>List of Students</h2>
@using (Html.BeginForm())
{
    @Html.AntiForgeryToken()
<p>
    <span>Filter by: </span>
    <select id="filterBy" name="filterBy">
        <option value="city">City</option>
        <option value="state">State</option>
        <option value="postalCode">Postal Code</option>
    </select>
    <span> = </span>
    <input type="text" id="filterValue" name="filterValue" />
</p>
<p>
    <span>Sort by: </span>
    <select id="sortBy" name="sortBy">
        <option value="firstName">First Name</option>
        <option value="lastName">Last Name</option>
    </select>
    <select id="sortOrder" name="sortOrder">
        <option value="asc">Ascending</option>
        <option value="desc">Descending</option>
    </select>
```

```
<input type="submit" value="Go" />
</p>
}
```
...

6. Open the StudentController.cs file from the
   Controllers folder, as shown in Figure 5-6. You
   need to add a new action in the controller to handle
   these new controls.

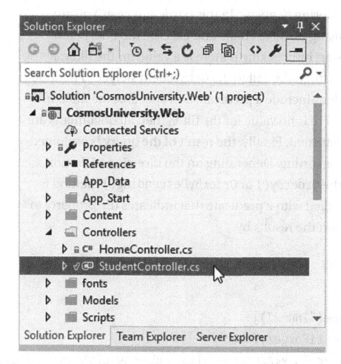

Figure 5-6. *Opening the StudentController.cs file from the Controllers folder*

7. Add the code in Listing 5-23 just after the Index() action finishes. The first thing to note in the new action is that, as opposed to the original Index() action, this will only accept POST requests. This is to prevent attacks using the URL. Then, there are four parameters that will contain the values entered in the page for filtering and sorting. The names of the parameters match the name property in all the HTML controls. The following lines are where the filtering happens. In this particular case, you are using LINQ to create and execute the query. You start by checking if there is a value for the filter; if so, then the call to the GetStudentsAsync() method does include a predicate that specifies the filter. If there is no value for the filter, then all documents are returned. Finally, the result of the query is evaluated for sorting. Depending on the direction of the sort, the OrderBy() or OrderByDescending() method is called with a predicate that indicates the property to sort the results by.

Listing 5-23. New Index( ) Action to Filter and Sort Results

```
[HttpPost]
[ActionName("Index")]
[ValidateAntiForgeryToken]
public async Task<ActionResult> IndexAsync(string filterBy,
            string filterValue, string sortBy,
            string sortOrder)
{
    IEnumerable<Student> students = null;
    if (!string.IsNullOrEmpty(filterValue))
    {
```

```csharp
    switch (filterBy)
    {
        case "city":
            students = await Repository<Student>
                .GetStudentsAsync(x => x.City == filterValue);
            break;
        case "state":
            students = await Repository<Student>
                .GetStudentsAsync(x => x.State == filterValue);
            break;
        case "postalCode":
            var postalCode = Convert.ToInt32(filterValue);
            students = await Repository<Student>
                .GetStudentsAsync(x => x.PostalCode == postalCode);
            break;
    }
}
else
{
    students = await Repository<Student>.GetStudentsAsync(null);
}

if (sortBy == "firstName")
{
    students = sortOrder == "asc"
                ? students.OrderBy(x => x.FirstName)
                : students.OrderByDescending(x => x.FirstName);
}
```

```
else
{
    students = sortOrder == "asc"
                  ? students.OrderBy(x => x.LastName)
                  : students.OrderByDescending(x => x.LastName);
}

return View(students);
}
```

8. At this point, you can compile and run the
   application. To test it, select the filter by city,
   enter the value Chicago, and click the Go button
   to perform the query. Note that this will produce
   the error shown in Figure 5-7. This error is caused
   because the collection you are querying is
   partitioned, and your query needs to look in different
   partitions because city is not the partition key and
   by default queries can only be performed in a single
   partition.

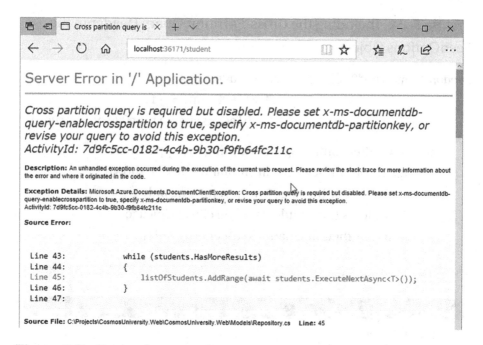

Figure 5-7. *Error when running a query on a partitioned collection*

9. The error message in Figure 5-7 is already telling you how to resolve this issue. You need to set the x-ms-documentdb-query-enablecrosspartition header to true in the call to the API. This will enable cross-partition queries. Since you are not using the REST API, you need to configure this header using the FeedOptions object that is passed in the CreateDocumentQuery() method in the repository. Listing 5-24 shows this adjustment.

Listing 5-24. Including the Cross-Partition Query Header in the
FeedOptions Object

```
FeedOptions feedOptions = new FeedOptions {
                          MaxItemCount = -1,
                          EnableCrossPartitionQuery = true };
```

10. Now, after compiling and running the application
     again you will see a result similar to the one shown
     in Figure 5-8. The page is now returning only
     documents from students in the city of Chicago
     sorted by their first name in ascending order.

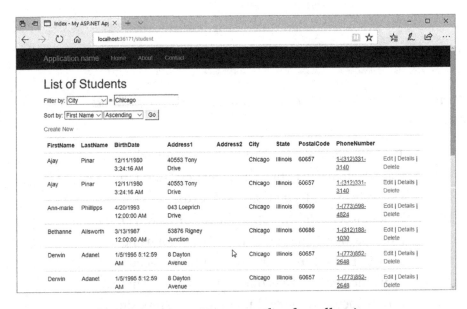

Figure 5-8. *Query now running correctly after allowing
cross-partition queries*

Implementing SQL Queries

Using SQL queries is very simple. For this purpose, you are going to create a new method in your repository class named GetStudentsSQLAsync() that will function the same as GetStudentsAsync(), only with the SQL syntax.

Listing 5-25 shows the code for this new method. Note that the signature of the method is different because it is expecting the values of the filter and sort as they are passed to the controller. These values will be used here to build the SQL query as a *string*. Also note that you keep the definition in the FeedOptions object to enable cross-partition queries. Then you start with the construction of the SELECT statement. An important distinction here is that since the client is communicating directly to a collection in the database, the name of the collection is not defined in the SELECT statement, only an alias. It is now the alias that is being used in the different clauses. Next, the WHERE clause is built using the filterBy and filterValue parameters. The filterBy parameter already contains the name of the property to be used as the filter, and the filterValue contains the actual value to use in the comparison. Finally, the SORT clause is created using the last two parameters. The rest of the method is similar to the previous GetStudentsAsync() method.

Listing 5-25. GetStudentsSQLAsync( ) Method Implementing SQL Syntax

```
public static async Task<IEnumerable<T>> GetStudentsSQLAsync(
                    string filterBy, string filterValue,
                    string sortBy, string sortOrder)
{
    Uri collectionUri = UriFactory.CreateDocumentCollectionUri(
                            _dbName, _collectionName);
```

```
FeedOptions feedOptions = new FeedOptions { MaxItemCount = -1,
                          EnableCrossPartitionQuery = true };

string sqlStatement = "SELECT * FROM s";
if (!string.IsNullOrEmpty(filterValue))
{
    string value = filterBy == "postalCode"
                   ? filterValue
                   : "'" + filterValue + "'";
    sqlStatement = sqlStatement + " WHERE s." + filterBy
                                        + " = " + value;
}

sqlStatement = sqlStatement + " ORDER BY s." + sortBy
                                  + " " + sortOrder.ToUpper();

IDocumentQuery<T> students =
            client.CreateDocumentQuery<T>(collectionUri,
                                  sqlStatement, feedOptions)
                      .AsDocumentQuery();

List<T> listOfStudents = new List<T>();
while (students.HasMoreResults)
{
    listOfStudents.AddRange(await students.
    ExecuteNextAsync<T>());
}

return listOfStudents;
}
```

To use the new method in Listing 5-25 you need to change the new Index( ) action in the controller. The modifications will basically eliminate all the coding for the Lambda query, as shown in Listing 5-26. Note that the call to the new method in the repository is all you need.

Listing 5-26. Calling GetStudentsSQLAsync( ) in the Controller

```
[HttpPost]
[ActionName("Index")]
[ValidateAntiForgeryToken]
public async Task<ActionResult> IndexAsync(string filterBy,
            string filterValue, string sortBy, string sortOrder)
{
    IEnumerable<Student> students = await
                    Repository<Student>.GetStudentsSQLAsync(
                                filterBy, filterValue,
                                sortBy, sortOrder);

    return View(students);
}
```

Implementing Parameterized Queries

The query in Listing 5-25 works well; however, it can be further enhanced by using parameters. For this, you need to change how the query is created. In this case, you need to create a SqlQuerySpec( ) object that will contain the string with the query as well as the parameters. See Listing 5-27 for the modified version of GetStudentsSQLAsync( ).

Listing 5-27. Implementing GetStudentsSQLAsync( ) with
Parameters

```
public static async Task<IEnumerable<T>> GetStudentsSQLAsync(
                        string filterBy, string filterValue,
                        string sortBy, string sortOrder)
{
    Uri collectionUri = UriFactory.CreateDocumentCollectionUri(
                            _dbName, _collectionName);
    FeedOptions feedOptions = new FeedOptions { MaxItemCount = -1,
                        EnableCrossPartitionQuery = true };

    string sqlStatement = "SELECT * FROM s";
    if (!string.IsNullOrEmpty(filterValue))
    {
        sqlStatement = sqlStatement
                + " WHERE s." + filterBy + " = @filterValue";
    }

    sqlStatement = sqlStatement + " ORDER BY s."
                        + sortBy + " " + sortOrder.ToUpper();

    SqlQuerySpec querySpec = new SqlQuerySpec()
    {
        QueryText = sqlStatement,
        Parameters = new SqlParameterCollection()
        {
```

```
        new SqlParameter("@filterValue", filterValue)
    }
};

IDocumentQuery<T> students =
            client.CreateDocumentQuery<T>(collectionUri,
                                querySpec, feedOptions)
                .AsDocumentQuery();

List<T> listOfStudents = new List<T>();
while (students.HasMoreResults)
{
    listOfStudents.AddRange(await
                        students.ExecuteNextAsync<T>());
}

    return listOfStudents;
}
```

Implementing LINQ Queries

Implementing LINQ queries is simple but has one particular issue worth
noting. Because LINQ works with specific objects and is strongly typed,
you can't really implement a generic T object as you have so far. In this
case, your sample method using LINQ will need to be strongly typed as
well, as you can see in Listing 5-28.

Listing 5-28. Implementing LINQ Queries in GetStudentsLINQAsync( )

```
public static async Task<IEnumerable<Student>>
                      GetStudentsLINQAsync(
                          string filterBy, string filterValue,
                          string sortBy, string sortOrder)
{
    Uri collectionUri =
              UriFactory.CreateDocumentCollectionUri(
                          _dbName, _collectionName);
    FeedOptions feedOptions = new FeedOptions { MaxItemCount = -1,
                          EnableCrossPartitionQuery = true };

    var linqQuery =
              from s in client.CreateDocumentQuery<Student>
                                  (collectionUri, feedOptions)
              select s;

    if (!string.IsNullOrEmpty(filterValue))
    {
        switch (filterBy)
        {
            case "city":
                linqQuery = from s in
                                  client.CreateDocumentQuery<Student>(
                                      collectionUri, feedOptions)
                              where s.City == filterValue
                              select s;
                break;
```

```
            case "state":
                linqQuery = from s in
                            client.CreateDocumentQuery<Student>(
                                collectionUri, feedOptions)
                            where s.State == filterValue
                            select s;
                break;
            case "postalCode":
                var postalCode = Convert.ToInt32(filterValue);
                linqQuery = from s in
                            client.CreateDocumentQuery<Student>(
                                collectionUri, feedOptions)
                            where s.PostalCode == postalCode
                            select s;
                break;
        }
}

if (sortBy == "firstName")
{
    linqQuery = sortOrder == "asc"
                ? linqQuery.OrderBy(x => x.FirstName)
                : linqQuery.OrderByDescending(x => x.FirstName);
}
else
{
    linqQuery = sortOrder == "asc"
                ? linqQuery.OrderBy(x => x.LastName)
                : linqQuery.OrderByDescending(x => x.LastName);
}
```

```
IDocumentQuery<Student> students = linqQuery.AsDocumentQuery();

List<Student> listOfStudents = new List<Student>();
while (students.HasMoreResults)
{
    listOfStudents.AddRange(await
                        students.ExecuteNextAsync<Student>());
}

    return listOfStudents;
}
```

Summary

In this chapter, you reviewed how indexing works and how it is configured. You learned how to change the index policy of a collection and the rules that guide these customizations. Then you went through the specifics of the SELECT statement and how is it used to query databases. You examined the four main clauses of the SELECT statement, which are SELECT, FROM, WHERE, and ORDER BY. You reviewed how with an addition to the FROM clause it is possible to iterate through the results of a query. Also, you examined how joins work and how they are similar and different than joins in relational databases. Later, you reviewed how parameterized SQL queries work and why they are important and you finished that section with a quick overview of the built-in functions implemented in Azure Cosmos DB.

The last part of the chapter was devoted to making a real implementation of all the techniques and concepts learned in the chapter. This was done by enhancing the sample application with the ability to refine the results presented in the page using filters on specific properties and sorting such results.

In the following chapter, I will talk in more detail about globally distributed databases and how to work with them to implement a system with automatic failover.

CHAPTER 6

Working with a Globally Distributed Database

Azure Cosmos DB is not only capable, but it's built from the ground up to be globally distributed. When the database is distributed across different regions, applications can be configured to take advantage of this, making them faster, scalable, and more resilient against data availability problems.

Configuring Global Distribution

One of the biggest advantages of global distribution is that the configuration happens in Azure and not the application itself. This greatly simplifies what the application needs to do to scale and perform at large scale.

To configure a database to be globally distributed, you only need to add more regions to the configuration. Azure will do the rest. The following steps will guide you through the process:

1. Log into the Azure portal using the account you created in Chapter 1 at https://portal.azure.com.

2. From the menu on the left, select Azure Cosmos DB.

© José Rolando Guay Paz 2018
J. R. Guay Paz, *Microsoft Azure Cosmos DB Revealed*,
https://doi.org/10.1007/978-1-4842-3351-1_6

3. If you do not have a database created and only see an empty list, you need to create a database. If you have one already, you can skip to step 4.

- Click the Add button at the top of the page to open the new database options page, shown in Figure 6-1.

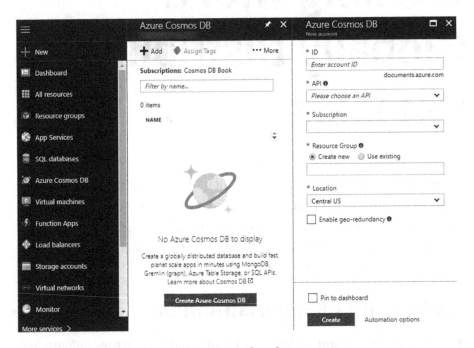

Figure 6-1. *New Azure Cosmos DB database page*

- The ID will indicate the name of your database. A green checkmark at the end of the box will indicate if the name you entered is globally unique.

- Now select the API you want to use. In your case, select *SQL (DocumentDB)*.

- Then select the subscription that you created previously, the one that is used for billing purposes.

- Now create a new resource group. The name of the resource group accepts letters, numbers, hyphens, and underscores. Again, a green checkmark at the end of the box will let you know everything is fine.

- Finally, select the location where this database should be created.

- The "Enable geo-redundancy" checkbox will allow you to automatically replicate the database to the associated geographically region of the selected region. This is called *region pairing*. Each region in Azure is paired with a second region that is located in the same geography (same country or continent). For example, for the *Central US* region shown in Figure 6-1, its paired region is *East US 2*. When selected, this checkbox effectively configures the database to be distributed with the selected region to be the write region and the paired region the read region.

4. Once you click the database name to open its properties, you need to click the *Replicate data globally* option, as shown in Figure 6-2.

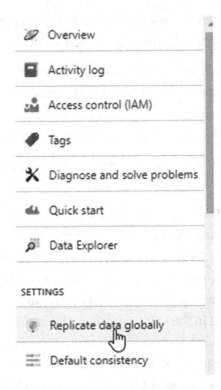

Figure 6-2. *Open the replication page to configure global distribution*

5. Once you click the *Replicate data globally* option,
    the Azure region map opens, as shown in Figure 6-3.
    This will show you where the Azure regions are in
    the world. You can replicate your database to any
    number of regions. All you have to do at this point
    is click each of the regions where you want your
    database. Each region is represented by a hexagon.

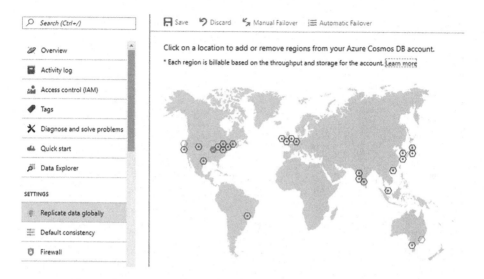

Figure 6-3. *Azure regions map for replication*

6. Once you have selected the regions, click the Save button at the top.

7. After Azure completes the configuration for replication, you should see something similar to Figure 6-4. Note that replicated regions are shown in a hexagon with solid blue background while the main region is shown in a light-blue hexagon.

Figure 6-4. *Azure Cosmos DB database replicated to multiple regions*

Configuring Failover

Failover is the operation that happens when a region is not available and the infrastructure switches to a backup region for service continuity. Azure Cosmos DB databases can failover manually or automatically. Figure 6-4 shows the two buttons at the top of the regions map: one for manual failover and one for automatic failover. Those two buttons are the ones that provide access to manually failover to a region or to configure automatic failover.

Working with Manual Failover

Manual failover is the default after you configure your database to replicate to at least one other region. With this setting, if the designated write region becomes unavailable, it is your responsibility to switch the database writes to a different region. You have the freedom to choose any region out of the set where the database is replicated.

Once you click the Manual Failover button, you will be presented with a page similar to the one shown in Figure 6-5. In it, you are presented with the current write region and the set of read regions.

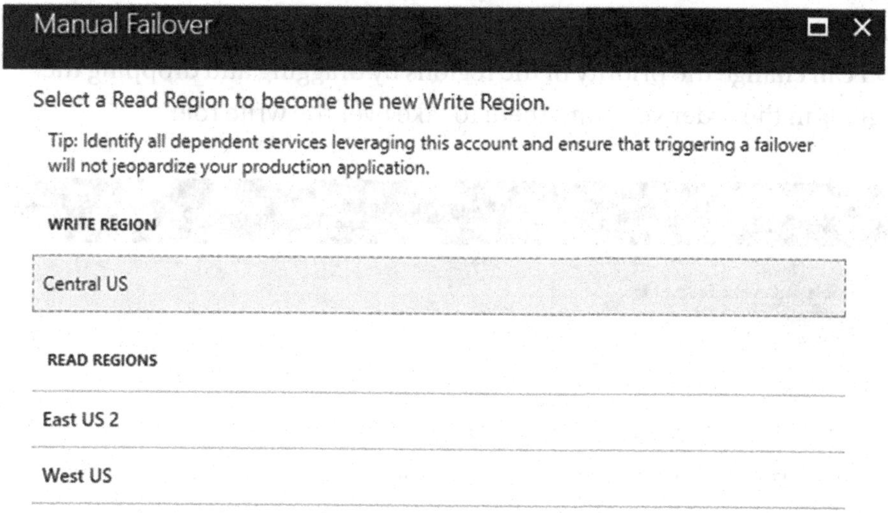

Figure 6-5. *Configuring manual failover*

To failover, all you need to do is select, out of the group of read regions, the one that will become the new write region. Click the checkbox to acknowledge that this is your intention and click the OK button at the bottom.

Configuring Automatic Failover

Let's now examine how automatic failover works. With this configuration, Azure will automatically switch the unavailable write region to a read region to become the new write region. Azure will know which region to choose based on the priority defined for the each of the read regions. You are only responsible for defining this priority and then Azure will do the rest.

Figure 6-6 shows the page that is opened when you click the `Automatic` `Failover` button. Similarly to the manual failover page, you are presented with the current write region and the list of read regions. What is different is that the read regions now have a priority column that tells Azure which one is the next to become the write region in the event of a region outage. You can change the priority of the regions by dragging and dropping the regions in the order you want them to take over the write role.

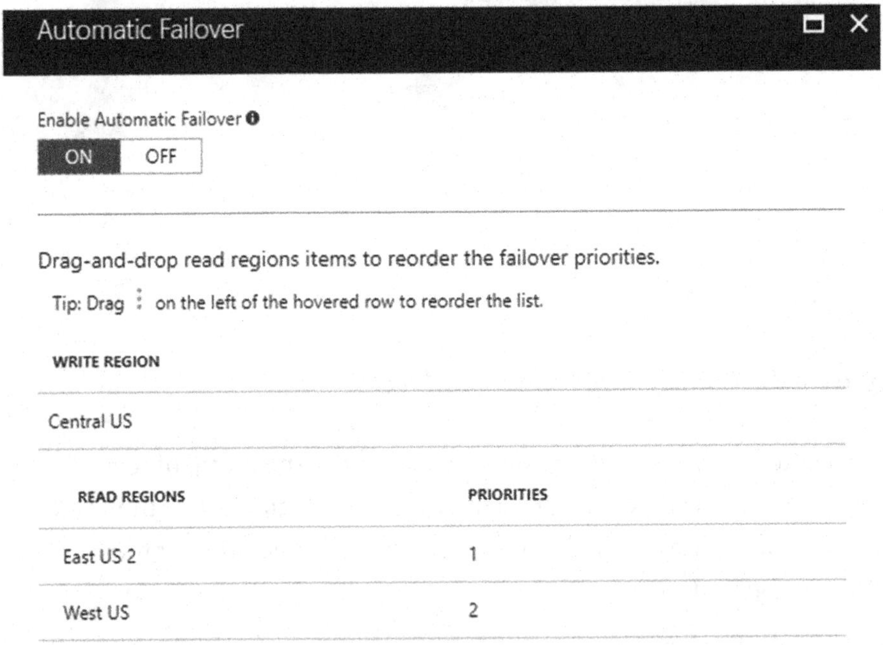

Automatic Failover   □ ✕

Enable Automatic Failover ❶

| ON | OFF |

Drag-and-drop read regions items to reorder the failover priorities.

Tip: Drag ⋮ on the left of the hovered row to reorder the list.

WRITE REGION

Central US

READ REGIONS	PRIORITIES
East US 2	1
West US	2

Figure 6-6. *Automatic failover priority*

In this example, the write region is *Central US*. If this region becomes unavailable, Azure will switch writes to the *East US 2* region. If the *East US 2* region becomes unavailable, Azure will switch writes to the *West US* region.

Connecting to a Preferred Region

The DocumentDB API allows you to programmatically configure the preferred order of regions in which document operations will be served. This configuration is done by setting the `PreferredLocations` collection in the `ConnectionPolicy` object that is passed to the `DocumentClient` object when it is initialized.

Another benefit of setting up the preferred regions list is that based on the Azure Cosmos DB account configuration, current regional availability, and the preference list specified, the most optimal endpoint will be chosen by the DocumentDB SDK to perform write and read operations.

When having a preferred regions list, all writes are sent to the current write region and reads are sent to the first region in the preferred regions list; if this region becomes unavailable, then the SDK redirects the requests to the next region in the list, and so on.

An important consideration is that if the database is replicated, for example, to five regions, but the preferred regions list only included four of them, then the last region will never serve requests, even if failover has chosen it to serve the requests. The preferred regions list defined in the application takes precedence over the failover Azure configuration.

To configure the connection policy to have a preferred region list, you need to define the regions in the `PreferredLocations` collection. In Listing 6-1 you can see the declaration and initialization of the `DocumentClient` object from the Cosmos University sample application you have been using. This code is located in the `/Models/Repository.cs` file, line 19.

Listing 6-1. Current DocumentClient Configuration in CosmosUniversity Sample app

```
private static ConnectionPolicy _connectionPolicy =
            new ConnectionPolicy {
                    EnableEndpointDiscovery = false
            };
private static DocumentClient client =
            new DocumentClient(new Uri(_endPoint),
                               _authKey,
                               _connectionPolicy);
```

Since the declaration is at the class level, you need to make a small modification to have a method of the repository class return the fully configured instance of the client. The new code is shown in Listing 6-2. Note that you now have a new method that creates the ConnectionPolicy object, configures it with the preferred regions list, and then returns a new instance of the DocumentClient object. The connection policy specifies that reads should be first served from the *Central US* region and then from the *West US 2* region.

Listing 6-2. Configuring the Preferred Regions List

```
private static DocumentClient client = GetNewDocumentClient();

private static DocumentClient GetNewDocumentClient()
{
    ConnectionPolicy _connectionPolicy =
                new ConnectionPolicy {
                    EnableEndpointDiscovery = false
            };
    _connectionPolicy.PreferredLocations
                    .Add(LocationNames.CentralUS);
```

```
_connectionPolicy.PreferredLocations
                   .Add(LocationNames.WestUS2);

return new DocumentClient(new Uri(_endPoint),
                    _authKey,
                    _connectionPolicy);
}
```

Implementing a Multi-Master Database

In general, having a single write region fits most application scenarios. However, there are cases when more write regions are needed to scale the application better. This configuration is known as multi-master.

Application Scenario

To explain this, imagine a scenario where a company has many offices across two continents (for example, America and Europe). This company has an application where thousands of users add, modify, and delete documents in an Azure Cosmos DB database. The configuration of the database includes a single write region in America with multiple read regions replicated in America and Europe. Users in Europe normally don't use information from America and vice versa, the only exception being the higher executives that need information from both places. To reduce latency and to provide an increased throughput it is determined that writes should happen on at least one region on each continent. Not only will this configuration make the application perform better, it can help with the expansion planned for the near future when the company starts operating in Asia.

The application is already deployed and working in multiple regions with an Azure traffic manager that routes traffic to the closest region to be served.

Implementing the Solution

Azure Cosmos Db does not provide writes to multiple regions out of the box. For this to work, you need to create two separate database accounts and configure the application to use them. This configuration is not exactly the same as you have seen before where Azure handles the data replication automatically. Instead, it will be the application's responsibility to read and write to the appropriate region depending on where the user is connecting from. Figure 6-7 shows the final architecture.

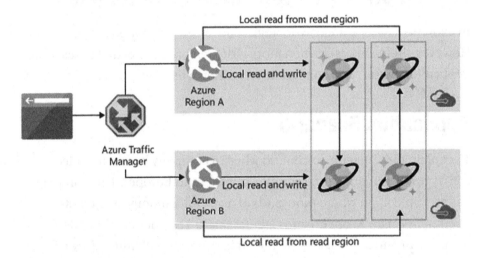

Figure 6-7. *Implementing multiple write regions (image taken from* `http://bit.ly/cosmos-db-multi-write)`

In this sample scenario, the database in America has a write region with multiple read regions; in Europe there is also a write region with multiple read regions. Now, you will add to the American database a read region in Europe, and in the same way the European database will have a read region in America. You want this to happen because Azure will replicate the information across continents automatically, and then the application will have both sets of information closer to the users who need them.

Now, let's imagine the write region in America is *East US* and it has a read region in *North Europe*. For the European database, its writes region is the *North Europe* region and the read region is *East US*. This configuration matches the architecture defined in Figure 6-7.

The application then needs to know what to do with this configuration. For this, you need to configure the region connection preference as described earlier in this chapter. Listing 6-3 shows how this configuration happens.

Listing 6-3. Configuring Connections to Multi-Write Regions

```
ConnectionPolicy writeClientPolicy =
        new ConnectionPolicy {
                ConnectionMode = ConnectionMode.Direct,
                ConnectionProtocol = Protocol.Tcp
        };
writeClientPolicy.PreferredLocations
                .Add(LocationNames.EastUS);
writeClientPolicy.PreferredLocations
                .Add(LocationNames.NorthEurope);

string americaDB = ConfigurationManager
                    .AppSettings["CosmosDBAmericaEndPoint"];
DocumentClient writeClient =
        new DocumentClient(new Uri(americaDB),
                            writeRegionAuthKey,
                            writeClientPolicy);

ConnectionPolicy readClientPolicy =
        new ConnectionPolicy {
                ConnectionMode = ConnectionMode.Direct,
                ConnectionProtocol = Protocol.Tcp
        };
```

```
readClientPolicy.PreferredLocations
                .Add(LocationNames.NorthEurope);
readClientPolicy.PreferredLocations
                .Add(LocationNames.EastUS);

string europeDB = ConfigurationManager
                    .AppSettings["CosmosDBEuropeEndPoint"];
DocumentClient readClient =
        new DocumentClient(new Uri(europeDB),
                        readRegionAuthKey,
                        readClientPolicy);
```

What you see in the code shown in Listing 6-3 is that the selected read and write regions will be determined by the preferred location list, but also by the traffic manager. In the case of American users, the selected read and write locations will be *East US*; for European users, the locations will be *North Europe*.

The application in this case will need to ensure that writes use the writeClient object and reads use the readClient object. Otherwise, the operations will not be done in the necessary regions.

With this, writes (add a new document, replace, or delete) will not require any code changes because the destination is already determined correctly. In the case of reads, if the queries require data from both continents, two individual query executions need to happen (one for each continent) and a manual merge of both results, as shown in Listing 6-4.

Listing 6-4. Querying from Two Different Databases

```
public async Task<IEnumerable<Doc>> ReadDocsAsync()
{
    IDocumentQuery<Document> writeAccount =
      (from d in
            writeClient.CreateDocumentQuery<Doc>
                        (this.contentCollection)
        select d).AsDocumentQuery();

    IDocumentQuery<Doc> readAccount =
      (from d in
            readClient.CreateDocumentQuery<Doc>
                        (this.contentCollection)
        select d).AsDocumentQuery();

    List<Doc> documents = new List<Doc>();

    while (writeAccount.HasMoreResults
                || readAccount.HasMoreResults)
    {
        IList<Task<FeedResponse<Doc>>> results =
                new List<Task<FeedResponse<Doc>>>();

        if (writeAccount.HasMoreResults)
        {
            results.Add(writeAccount.ExecuteNextAsync<Doc>());
        }

        if (readAccount.HasMoreResults)
        {
            results.Add(readAccount.ExecuteNextAsync<Doc>());
        }
```

```
        IList<FeedResponse<Doc>> docFeedResult =
                            await Task.WhenAll(results);

        foreach (FeedResponse<Doc> feed in docFeedResult)
        {
            documents.AddRange (feed);
        }
    }
    return documents;
}
```

Summary

In this chapter, you reviewed in detail the global distribution characteristics of Azure Cosmos DB. You learned, step by step, how to use the Azure portal to replicate a database to different regions. Then you examined failover and how to configure manual and automatic failover for your database so application continuity is guaranteed even in the event of region outages. The chapter ended by describing how to connect to a preferred location and the configuration changes necessary for an application that needs to have multiple write regions.

CHAPTER 7

Advanced Concepts

When working with Azure Cosmos DB, there are several concepts that, while they are familiar if you are coming from a relational database, they will look completely alien. This is because they are implemented in a different language or syntax. For example, to create stored procedures, triggers, and user-defined functions you use the JavaScript language. The implementation of JavaScript is based on the ECMAScript 2015 specification (you can find more about this specification at www.ecma-international.org/ecma-262/6.0/).

You will examine how to properly create and execute these elements. In addition, you will see how to work with dates in JSON documents and you will learn some tips for backing up, restoring, and testing the performance of a database.

Working with Transactions

Transactions are a typical and extremely important concept in relational databases. A transaction is a set of operations that change the data stored in the database in some way, but for these changes to persists, all operations must succeed. In the event of a failure in any operation, all other operations must roll back their changes to leave the data intact. A successful transaction normally ends with a commit command that

© José Rolando Guay Paz 2018
J. R. Guay Paz, *Microsoft Azure Cosmos DB Revealed*,
https://doi.org/10.1007/978-1-4842-3351-1_7

confirms the success and instructs the database to make all data changes permanent. Unsuccessful transactions issue a rollback command that undoes all data changes and returns the data to its original state.

In Azure Cosmos DB, transactions fully support *ACID* (atomicity, consistency, isolation, and durability). These four terms define the guarantees for transactions to maintain the integrity of the data. *Atomicity* defines that all operations are executed as a single unit. They all need to be executed and all must succeed or none at all. *Consistency* refers to the guarantee that data will be in a valid state between transactions. *Isolation* makes sure that data being used within a transaction cannot be modified by any other transaction until it is committed or rolled back. *Durability* ensures that data changes are permanent once the transaction is committed.

As mentioned, stored procedures and triggers are created using JavaScript. This server-side JavaScript code is stored and executed in the same memory space where the database is running. This fact is what allows Azure Cosmos DB to guarantee ACID for all operations that are part of a single stored procedure or trigger. This is a very important consideration and distinction of Azure Cosmos DB. Furthermore, *a stored procedure or trigger is implicitly considered a transaction and the successful execution of it constitutes an implicit commit whereas throwing an error performs an automatic rollback.*

Implementing Stored Procedures

A stored procedure consists of a JavaScript *function* and an *id* that identifies it. Within the function, there are several objects that give access to the execution `context`, the `request` sent to the server, the `response` that will be sent back to the client, and the `collection` being accessed.

To illustrate the implementation, let's create a stored procedure that will replace the current functionality for creating student documents in the sample application. Listing 7-1 shows the code of the stored procedure.

Listing 7-1. Stored Procedure to Create a New Student Document

```
/*
* createStudent: Stored procedure to create a new student
  document in an Azure Cosmos DB database
*
* @param {student} student - The student document being created.
*
*/
function createStudent(student) {
      // Get the context, collection and response objects
      var context = getContext();
      var collection = context.getCollection();
      var response = context.getResponse();

      // Get the Uri to the collection
      var collectionLink = collection.getSelfLink();

      // Call the function to insert the new student
      // document in the collection
      insertDoc(student, function(error, studentDoc){
                      if (error) throw error;

                      var responseBody = {
                              student : studentDoc
                      };

                      response.setBody(responseBody);
            })

      // Function to create the new student document
      // in the collection
      function insertDoc(student, callback) {
```

```
            var options = {
                    disableAutomaticIdGeneration : false
            };

            var wasCreated = collection
                        .createDocument(collectionLink,
                        student, options,
                        function(err, doc) {
                                callback(err, doc);
                        }
        );

        if (!wasCreated){
                throw new
                        Error("Student could not be created");
        }
    }
}
```

Let's examine this function in detail. The function accepts as a parameter the student document that is passed from the application with the student information.

In the first part of the function you get access to the three objects you are interested in. They are the context object, which provides access to all the operations that can be performed in the Azure Cosmos DB database. From the context object you then get the collection you are working on and the response that will be sent back to the client. The collection is defined by the client application at the time of connection.

```
// Get the context, collection and response objects
var context = getContext();
var collection = context.getCollection();
var response = context.getResponse();
```

The following part is the call to a second function that handles the actual data manipulation. You are sending two pieces of information: the student document and a callback function. The reason this is done this way is to have control of the execution flow.

In JavaScript, functions are of type object, which makes it possible to pass them as parameters. This concept is taken from a programming paradigm called *functional programming*. The callback function can be called inside the function where it was passed as a parameter. Using callback functions makes it easy to define what will happen after the principal function has completed its execution. If the callback function is not called, then it just won't do anything. If you didn't have callback functions, you would need to expect some return value from the function, evaluate it, and determine whether or not to execute some additional code. With this mechanism, the callback function is used if needed and that is determined from within the principal function.

```
// Call the function to insert the new student
// document in the collection
insertDoc(student,
            function(error, studentDoc){
                if (error) throw error;

                var responseBody = {
                        student : studentDoc
                };

                response.setBody(responseBody);
        })
```

The purpose of this particular callback function is to evaluate whether there has been an error when adding the new document to the collection. In the event of an error, nothing will happen and an automatic rollback will be issued. If there is no error, then a JSON response is built with the student document, which is then sent back to the client using the setBody() function of the response object.

The final part of the stored procedure is the internal function that adds the document in the collection. The first thing you need to do is create a CreateOptions object that will provide the necessary settings to handle ids. In this case, because the application is not generating its own ids but it is relying on Azure Cosmos DB to do so, you need to override the document creation default behavior, which is to not to generate an id for the document. This is done by setting the disableAutomaticIdGeneration setting to false.

Next, you call the createDocument() method from the collection object. This method will return true if the document was successfully added to the collection and false otherwise. The code passes four parameters: the collection Uri so it knows where to create the document, the actual document, and the creation options. The last parameter is an anonymous function that will be called after the method execution. This function will take two parameters: an error object if something happened that prevented the document creation and the document being inserted. This function will run the callback function that was passed to the insertdoc() function.

If the createDocument() method failed for any reason, it will return false as noted earlier and you capture that value in the wasCreated variable. You evaluate this variable later and if it did not succeed then the function will throw an error.

```
// Function to create the new student document
// in the collection
function insertDoc(student, callback) {
    var options = {
        disableAutomaticIdGeneration : false
    };

    var wasCreated  = collection.createDocument(collectionLink,
        student, options,
```

```
        function(err, doc) {
            callback(err, doc);
        }
    );

    if (!wasCreated){
        throw new Error("Student could not be created");
    }
}
```

Creating a Stored Procedure

There are two ways to create a stored procedure. The first one is using the Azure portal. The second one is programmatically using the SDK.

Creating a Stored Procedure in the Azure Portal

Using the Azure portal is very straightforward. Open the Data Explorer from the menu on the left. Then click the collection name and from there click the New Stored Procedure at the top, as shown in Figure 7-1.

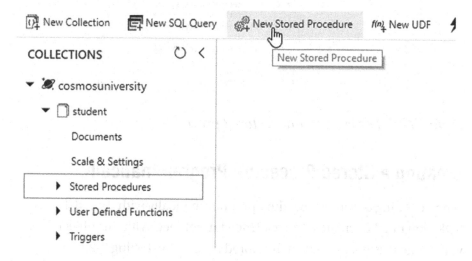

Figure 7-1. *Creating a new stored procedure*

You are now presented with a textbox to enter the stored procedure id and a text area where you will type the JavaScript function that is executed when calling the stored procedure. Note that the id of the stored procedure can be named differently than the function; while this is valid, I recommend naming them the same to keep consistency and avoid confusion later.

Now type createStudent for the id of the stored procedure and type in the code from Listing 7-1, as shown in Figure 7-2. Once everything is entered, click the Save button.

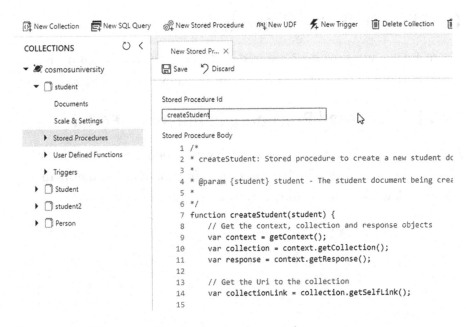

Figure 7-2. *The createStudent stored procedure*

Creating a Stored Procedure Programmatically

When creating a stored procedure programmatically with the .NET SDK, you need to create a StoredProcedure object. With this object, you define the id and body of the stored procedure. Listing 7-2

shows how the object is created. All you need to do next is call the
CreateStoredProcedureAsync() method which accepts two parameters:
the collection Uri and the stored procedure object. As you can see in the
code, the stored procedure body is defined as a string passed to the Body
property of the object. While this can be done, you might lose certain
capabilities of the editor in the Azure portal such as IntelliSense and color
highlighting for keywords. It will depend on what environment you feel
more comfortable with.

Listing 7-2. Creating a Stored Procedure Programmatically

```
var createStudentSProc = new StoredProcedure
{
    Id = "createStudent",
    Body = @"
/*
* createStudent: Stored procedure to create
*        a new student document in an Azure Cosmos DB database
*
* @param {student} student:
*                   The student document being created.
*/
function createStudent(student) {
    // Get the context, collection and response objects
    var context = getContext();
    var collection = context.getCollection();
    var response = context.getResponse();

    // Get the Uri to the collection
    var collectionLink = collection.getSelfLink();

        // Call the function to insert the new student
```

```
        // document in the collection
        insertDoc(student, function(error, studentDoc){
                        if (error) throw error;

                        var responseBody = {
                                student : studentDoc
                        };

                        response.setBody(responseBody);
                })

        // Function to create the new student document
        // in the collection
        function insertDoc(student, callback) {
                var options = {
                        disableAutomaticIdGeneration : false
                };

                var wasCreated  = collection
                        .createDocument(collectionLink,
                                student,
                                options,
                                function(err, doc) {
                                        callback(err, doc);
                                });

                if (!wasCreated){
                        throw new
                                Error("Student could not be created");

                }
        }
}"
};
```

```
// create the stored procedure in the collection
Uri collectionUri =
    UriFactory.CreateDocumentCollectionUri
                        (_dbName, _collectionName);

StoredProcedure createdStoredProcedure =
    await client.CreateStoredProcedureAsync
                        (collectionUri,
                            createStudentSProc);
```

Executing a Stored Procedure

Let's now use the stored procedure you created in the sample application. Open the application in Visual Studio and then open the Repository.cs file located in the Models folder. You will add a new async method called CreateStudentWithStoredProcAsync() that will accept a parameter that represents the student document. This method is shown in Listing 7-3. The definition of the method is very similar to the CreateStudentAsync() one.

Listing 7-3. Calling a Stored Procedure Using the .NET SDK

```
public static async Task<Document>
                    CreateStudentWithStoredProcAsync(T student)
{
    Uri storedProcedureUri =
            UriFactory.CreateStoredProcedureUri
                        (_dbName,
                        _collectionName,
                        "createStudent");

    var st = student as Student;

    RequestOptions requestOptions = new RequestOptions
    {
        PartitionKey = new PartitionKey(st.PostalCode)
    };
```

```
return await
       client.ExecuteStoredProcedureAsync<Document>
                    (storedProcedureUri,
                     requestOptions,
                     student);
}
```

The first thing you need to do is get the Uri of the stored procedure. This is done using the CreateStoredProcedureUri() method from the UriFactory class. This method will take three parameters: the database, collection, and stored procedure names.

The following step is to create a RequestOptions object to define the partition key from your collection. This is done by reading the postal code property from the student document. If the collection doesn't have a partition key, this can be omitted.

Finally, the stored procedure is executed by calling the ExecuteStoredProcedureAsync() asynchronous method. This method takes three parameters: the stored procedure Uri, the RequestOptions object, and the new document to be inserted.

Now you need to adjust the controller to call this new method instead of the CreateStudentAsync() method currently being used. For this, open the StudentController.cs file in the Controllers folder.

Find the CreateAsync() action method and replace the call to CreateStudentAsync() with CreateStudentWithStoredProcAsync(), as shown in Listing 7-4.

Listing 7-4. Creating an Action Method in StudentController.cs

```
// POST: Student/Create
[HttpPost]
[ActionName("Create")]
[ValidateAntiForgeryToken]
```

```
public async Task<ActionResult> CreateAsync(Student student)
{
    if (!ModelState.IsValid)
        return View(student);

    try
    {
        Repository<Student>
            .CreateStudentWithStoredProcAsync(student);

        return RedirectToAction("Index");
    }
    catch
    {
        return View(student);
    }
}
```

After these modifications, compile and run the application. It will behave exactly as before but now it will use the stored procedure to create new documents into the database.

Implementing Triggers

In Azure Cosmos DB, a trigger is similar to a stored procedure in the sense that it is a JavaScript function with an id; however, triggers are different in their execution because they run before or after a data manipulation operation (create, update, or delete).

Similar to stored procedures, triggers have access to the Context object but contrary to them, they cannot take any parameters. Triggers that run before the data operation are called *pre-triggers* and those that run after the operation are called *post-triggers*.

Pre-triggers have access to the request object and post-triggers have access to the response object. Also, both pre-triggers and post-triggers run within the same transaction context as the operation they are bound to. This is important because any error thrown by the triggers will halt the operation and roll back any modifications that have been made.

A big difference between Azure Cosmos DB triggers and relational database triggers is that, as opposed as relational databases, triggers in Azure Cosmos DB are optional and must be specified on each operation. This is done for performance reasons but also to reduce the RUs required for the operations. The way to include triggers in the execution of operations is by adding them to the RequestOptions object.

Let's look at an example. Imagine you have a request in which you need to identify students that can be considered geniuses. For this purpose, the criterion is to find out if a student is 15 years old or younger. You want to do this in a way that every student is evaluated and a field is set to true. Listing 7-5 illustrates a trigger that does this. Note that this calculation for age does not take daylight savings or different time zones, therefore it may not be 100% accurate on some extreme cases.

Listing 7-5. Trigger to Identify If a Student is 15 Years Old or Younger

```
function preCreateStudentIdentifyGenius(){
    var context = getContext();
    var request = context.getRequest();

    // student document to be created in the current operation
    var doc = request.getBody();

    // Find age of student
    var birthDate = new Date(doc.birthDate);
    var ageDifMs = Date.now() - birthDate.getTime();
    var ageDate = new Date(ageDifMs);
    var age = Math.abs(ageDate.getUTCFullYear() - 1970);
```

```
// Verify if the student is 15 years old or younger
if (age <= 15) {
    doc.genius = true;
}

// update the document that will be created
request.setBody(doc);
}
```

The trigger is getting the context and request objects at the beginning. With the request object you have access to the request body using the getBody() method. The getBody() method will return the JSON document representing the entity you are working on, which in this case is a student document.

Then the trigger attempts to calculate the age of the student based on the birth date, which is then used to evaluate if he or she is 15 years old or younger. If so, a new property is added to the document indicating the student is a genius.

Finally, the modified document is saved back to the body of the request so it can be processed later.

After this is in place, you can modify the client to include the trigger in the operation so it gets called. Listing 7-6 shows the adjustment to the RequestOptions object.

Listing 7-6. Including a Trigger for Execution in the RequestOptions Object

```
RequestOptions requestOptions = new RequestOptions {
    PreTriggerInclude =
            new List<string>
                { "preCreateStudentIdentifyGenius" }
};
```

Creating a Trigger

Triggers, similar to stored procedures, can be created either in the Azure portal or programmatically.

Creating a Trigger in the Azure Portal

To create a trigger in the Azure portal, open the Data Explorer from the menu and then click the collection. From the menu at the top, click the New Trigger button shown in Figure 7-3.

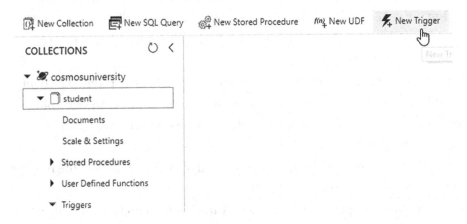

Figure 7-3.   *Creating a trigger from the Azure portal*

This opens a new page with a textbox to type the name of the trigger. You then need to select if it is a pre- or post-trigger in the *Trigger Type* drop-down. Then you select whether the trigger should fire for all operations or for one of create, delete, or replace. Finally, at the bottom is the area to type in the trigger function. This is shown in Figure 7-4. Note that in this figure I have selected a pre-trigger that is going to run before creating documents. Once everything is ready, just click the Save button.

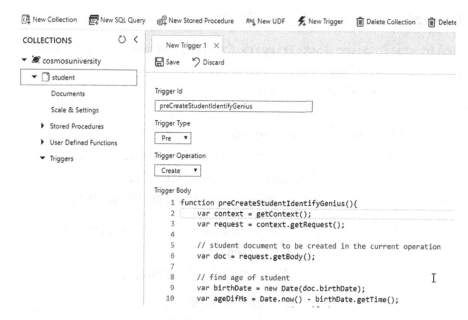

Figure 7-4. Configuring a trigger

Creating a Trigger Programmatically

To programmatically create a trigger, you need to use a `Trigger` object. This object has the same properties as in the Azure portal. You will have to define the `id` of the trigger; the trigger function is passed as a string in the `Body` property. The type of trigger is passed in the `TriggerType` property which accepts values from the `TriggerType` enumeration that has two possible values: `Pre` or `Post`. The trigger operation is passed in the `TriggerOperation` property that accepts values from the `TriggerOperation` enumeration which contains values for `All`, `Create`, `Delete`, `Replace`, and `Update`. Listing 7-7 shows a method that creates a trigger programmatically.

Once the `Trigger` object is created, you create the `Uri` of the collection where the trigger will be added. Then you need to call the `CreateTriggerAsync()` method that takes two parameters. The first one is the collection `Uri` and the second one is the `Trigger` object.

Listing 7-7. Creating a Trigger Programmatically

```csharp
public static async Task<Trigger> CreateAzureCosmosDBTriggerAsync()
{
    var createTrigger = new Trigger
    {
        Id = "preCreateStudentIdentifyGenius",
        Body = @"function preCreateStudentIdentifyGenius(){
                    var context = getContext();
                    var request = context.getRequest();

                    // student document to be created in
                    // the current operation
                    var doc = request.getBody();

                    // find age of student
                    var birthDate = new Date(doc.birthDate);
                    var ageDifMs = Date.now()
                                        - birthDate.getTime();
                    var ageDate = new Date(ageDifMs);
                    var age = Math.abs(
                                ageDate.getUTCFullYear()- 1970);

                    // Verify if the student is
                    // 15 years old or younger
                    if (age <= 15) {
                            doc.genius = true;
                    }

                    // update the document that will be created
                    request.setBody(doc);
                }",
        TriggerType = TriggerType.Pre,
        TriggerOperation = TriggerOperation.Create
    };
```

```
Uri collectionUri =
        UriFactory.CreateDocumentCollectionUri
            (_dbName, _collectionName);

    return await
        client.CreateTriggerAsync
                (collectionUri, createTrigger);
}
```

Implementing User-Defined Functions

A user-defined function (UDF) in Azure Cosmos DB is a JavaScript function that can be used to implement simple business logic. UDFs don't have access to the context object and can only be used inside queries. This is a huge distinction from stored procedures and triggers, and it has an important implication because it means that UDFs can only be run on read regions.

Let's now create a UDF that can help you in your sample application. In your application you list all the students and show all the properties stored in the database. Let's create a new page where you will see only the first and last name of the students and their age. In this case, you have the student's birthdate but not the age, so let's create a UDF that can calculate it.

The code for this function is in Listing 7-8.

Listing 7-8. UDF to Calculate the Age of a Student Based on Birthdate

```
function studentAge (studentBirthDate) {
    var birthDate = new Date(studentBirthDate);
    var ageDifMs = Date.now() - birthDate.getTime();
    var ageDate = new Date(ageDifMs);
    var age = Math.abs(ageDate.getUTCFullYear() - 1970);

    return age;
}
```

For this calculation you're taking the code used in Listing 7-5 to calculate the age of a student. Note that in the function there is no context object and it only contains JavaScript functions.

Creating a UDF

To add the UDF to the collection, similar to stored procedures and triggers, there are two options: using the Azure portal and programmatically.

Creating a UDF in the Azure Portal

To add a new UDF using the Azure portal, click in Data Explorer from the left menu and then click *New UDF* at the top of the page, as shown in Figure 7-5.

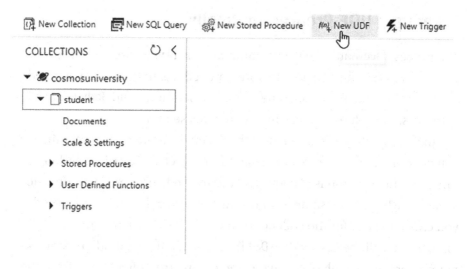

Figure 7-5. *Creating a UDF using the Azure portal*

After you click the New UDF button, a new page opens up with two fields to fill. The first one is the UDF id and the second one is the function that will be executed. As you can see in Figure 7-6, enter studentAge in the Id field; in the function body field, type the code from Listing 7-8.

```
1  function studentAge (studentBirthDate) {
2      var birthDate = new Date(studentBirthDate);
3      var ageDifMs = Date.now() - birthDate.getTime();
4      var ageDate = new Date(ageDifMs);
5      var age = Math.abs(ageDate.getUTCFullYear() - 1970);
6
7      return age;
8  }
9
```

Figure 7-6. *Creating the studentAge UDF*

Creating a UDF Programmatically

The process to create a UDF programmatically is very similar to the one you saw for creating a trigger or stored procedure. In this case, you need to use a UserDefinedFunction object and you set the Id and Body properties with the same values you saw in the previous section.

In Listing 7-9, you can see how this is implemented. The first thing you do is create the UserDefinedFunction object as described earlier. The Id of the function is studentAge and the Body property contains the function, which is the same as in Listing 7-8. Once the object is created, you create the Uri for the collection where the UDF will be stored. Finally, you call the CreateUserDefinedFunction() method, passing as parameters the two objects you created before: the collection Uri and the UserDefinedFunction object.

Listing 7-9. Method to Create a UDF Programmatically

```
public static async Task<UserDefinedFunction> createUDF()
{
    var createUDF = new UserDefinedFunction
    {
        Id = "studentAge",
        Body = @"function studentAge (studentBirthDate) {
                    var birthDate = new Date(studentBirthDate);
                    var ageDifMs = Date.now() - birthDate.getTime();
                    var ageDate = new Date(ageDifMs);
                    var age = Math.abs(ageDate.getUTCFullYear()- 1970);

                    return age;
                }"
    };
```

```
Uri collectionUri =
  UriFactory.CreateDocumentCollectionUri(
  _dbName, _collectionName);

  return await
          client.CreateUserDefinedFunctionAsync(
                     collectionUri, createUDF);
}
```

Using a UDF

Now that you have created a UDF, you are going to continue with the scenario and implement the new page in your sample application to list the names and ages of the students.

The first thing you need to do is add a new method to the Repository class where you will be querying the database to get the properties you want from the collection. In addition, the query will use the UDF you just created to populate a new property called studentAge. I'm assuming at this point the sample application is open in Visual Studio.

Open the Repository.cs file from the Models folder. You are going to create a new async method named GetStudentsAgeAsync(). The method will not accept any parameters. The method's code is shown in Listing 7-10.

Listing 7-10. GetStudentsAgeAsync() Method in the Repository Class

```
public static async Task<IEnumerable<T>> GetStudentsAgeAsync()
{
    Uri collectionUri =
        UriFactory.CreateDocumentCollectionUri(
                                    _dbName, _collectionName);
    FeedOptions feedOptions = new FeedOptions {
```

```csharp
                                MaxItemCount = -1,
                                EnableCrossPartitionQuery = true
                };

    string sqlStatement =
                @"SELECT s.firstName, s.lastName,
                    udf.studentAge(s.birthDate) AS studentAge
                FROM s";

    SqlQuerySpec querySpec = new SqlQuerySpec()
    {
        QueryText = sqlStatement,
    };

    IDocumentQuery<T> students =
                client.CreateDocumentQuery<T>(collectionUri,
                querySpec, feedOptions).AsDocumentQuery();

    List<T> listOfStudents = new List<T>();
    while (students.HasMoreResults)
    {
        listOfStudents.AddRange(
                    await students.ExecuteNextAsync<T>());
    }

    return listOfStudents;
}
```

The code implements a SQL query where you read the `firstName` and `lastName` properties from the documents in the collection. In addition, you've added a call to the UDF, passing as a parameter the `birthDate` property. Note that for calling UDFs you will need to use the `udf.` prefix. If you don't use the prefix, you will get an error because this is how Azure Cosmos DB identifies the function as a UDF. The rest of the code is very similar to the method built in Listing 5-25 in Chapter 5, which implements a query to the database using SQL syntax.

What follows is to create a new class that will represent this reduced version of the `Student.cs` class that you created in Chapter 3. The class will contain only three properties: the first name, last name, and age of a student. The following steps will guide you through the process of adding this class:

1.   Right-click in the `Models` folder in the Solution
     Explorer window. From the context menu, select
     Add and then *Class*, as shown in Figure 7-7.

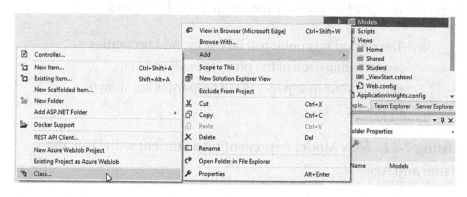

Figure 7-7. *Adding a new class in the Models folder for your document*

2. When the Add New Item window opens, type the
    name of the file as StudentAge.cs and click the Add
    button, as shown in Figure 7-8.

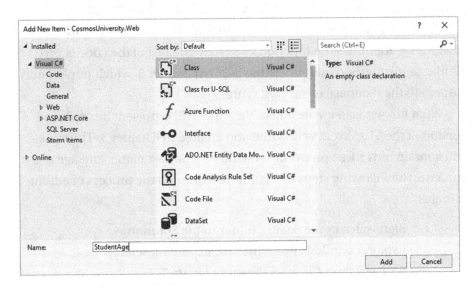

Figure 7-8. *Creating a new class named StudentAge.cs*

3. The class at this point will be empty. Add properties
    representing each of the properties you want to
    show in your new page. These properties are shown
    in Listing 7-11.

Listing 7-11. New Model Representing a Student with Only the
Name and Age

```
using System;
using System.Collections.Generic;
using System.Linq;
using System.Web;
```

```
namespace CosmosUniversity.Web.Models
{
    public class StudentAge
    {
        public string Id { get; set; }
        public string FirstName { get; set; }
        public string LastName { get; set; }
        public int StudentAge { get; set; }
    }
}
```

4. As you saw in Chapter 3, the names of the properties in the class use Pascal Case notation while the JSON document uses Camel Case. This might cause some problems but they are easily solved by adding annotations to match the casing between both formats. To make these annotations, you will need to add the `Newtonsoft.Json` namespace to the class, as shown in Listing 7-12.

Listing 7-12. StudentAge Model Now with Annotations in the Class Properties to Match the JSON Document's Camel Case

```
using Newtonsoft.Json;
using System;
using System.Collections.Generic;
using System.Linq;
using System.Web;

namespace CosmosUniversity.Web.Models
{
    public class StudentAge
    {
```

```
[JsonProperty(PropertyName = "id")]
public string Id { get; set; }

[JsonProperty(PropertyName = "firstName")]
public string FirstName { get; set; }

[JsonProperty(PropertyName = "lastName")]
public string LastName { get; set; }

[JsonProperty(PropertyName = "studentAge")]
public int StudentAge { get; set; }
    }
}
```

5. The next step is to add an action method in the student controller. Open the StudentController.cs file in the Controllers folder. The code of the action method is similar to the IndexAsync() method but it uses the StudentAge model you created. The code of the method is in Listing 7-13.

Listing 7-13. AgeList Action Method

```
[ActionName("AgeList")]
public async Task<ActionResult> AgeListAsync()
{
    var students = await Repository<StudentAge>.GetStudentsAgeAsync();
    return View(students);
}
```

In Listing 7-13 you are calling the GetStudentsAgeAsync() method from the Repository class and passing the results to the view for rendering to the client.

6. The final step is to create the view that will render the results to the user. From the AgeList action method, right-click the top of the View(students) code and select Add View, as shown in Figure 7-9. This will open the Add View window shown in Figure 7-10.

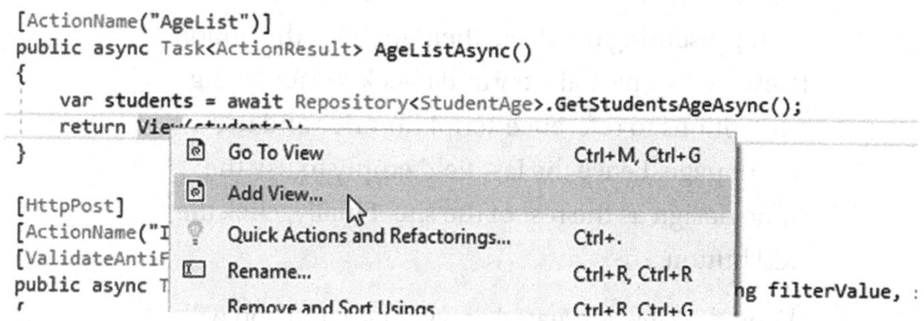

```
[ActionName("AgeList")]
public async Task<ActionResult> AgeListAsync()
{
    var students = await Repository<StudentAge>.GetStudentsAgeAsync();
    return View(students);
}

[HttpPost]
[ActionName("I
[ValidateAntiF
public async T                                                   ng filterValue, :
```

	Go To View	Ctrl+M, Ctrl+G
	Add View...	
	Quick Actions and Refactorings...	Ctrl+.
	Rename...	Ctrl+R, Ctrl+R
	Remove and Sort Usings	Ctrl+R, Ctrl+G

Figure 7-9. *Adding a view to render the results of the AgeList action method*

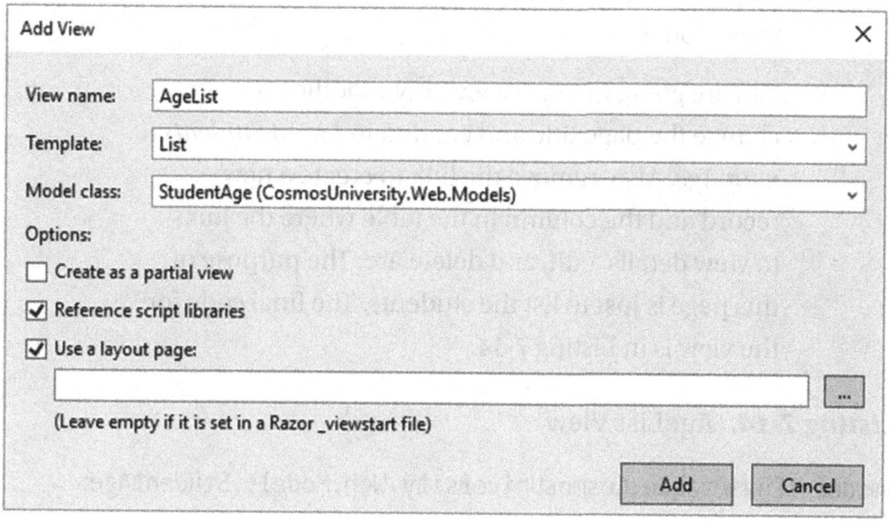

Figure 7-10. *The Add View window*

7. In the Add View window, type AgeList in the view
    name field. Select List for the template because you
    want to show a list of records. For this template to
    work, you need to identify the Model class. Select
    from the list StudentAge (CosmosUniversity.Web.
    Models). This is the class you created earlier to use
    for representing the data. Then uncheck the option
    to create as a partial view and check the following
    two options to reference script libraries and use a
    layout page. Leave the last field empty to use the
    same design as the rest of the site. Finally, click the
    Add button.

8. When the view is created, it will open and you will
    see it is a simple table with headers automatically
    using the name of the fields they represent and a for
    loop to iterate over all of the records returned in the
    view model.

9. You are going to make a few tiny modifications to
    change the page title and caption to *List of Students
    with Age*. Also, remove the link to create a new
    record and the column in the table where the links
    to view details, edit, and delete are. The purpose of
    this page is just to list the students. The final code for
    the view is in Listing 7-14.

Listing 7-14. AgeList View

```
@model IEnumerable<CosmosUniversity.Web.Models.StudentAge>

@{
    ViewBag.Title = "List of Students with Age";
}
```

```html
<h2>List of Students with Age</h2>

<table class="table">
    <tr>
        <th>
            @Html.DisplayNameFor(model => model.FirstName)
        </th>
        <th>
            @Html.DisplayNameFor(model => model.LastName)
        </th>
        <th>
            @Html.DisplayNameFor(model => model.Age)
        </th>
    </tr>

@foreach (var item in Model) {
    <tr>
        <td>
            @Html.DisplayFor(modelItem => item.FirstName)
        </td>
        <td>
            @Html.DisplayFor(modelItem => item.LastName)
        </td>
        <td>
            @Html.DisplayFor(modelItem => item.Age)
        </td>
    </tr>
}

</table>
```

10. Once you save the modifications for the view, compile and run the application. To open this new page, use the `http://localhost:[port]/Student/AgeList` URL. In the URL, use the port Visual Studio assigned in your environment. You should see a result similar to the one shown in Figure 7-11.

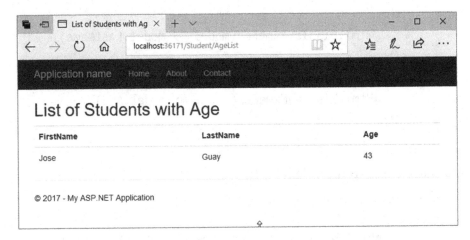

Figure 7-11. *Result of the query using a UDF to calculate the age of students*

Working with Dates

In Azure Cosmos DB, dates are serialized as strings using the ISO 8601 format. There is no native data type for DateTime as there is in relational databases. This is because Azure Cosmos DB implements the native JSON data model in which there are six basic types (string, number, boolean, array, object, and null). Fortunately, JSON is flexible enough to represent complex data types from these primitives, composing them as objects or arrays.

The fact that dates are serialized as strings should not be considered a concern. There are several benefits.

- Strings can be compared, and the relative ordering of the DateTime values is preserved when they are transformed to strings.

- This approach doesn't require any custom code or attributes for JSON conversion.

- The dates as stored in JSON are human readable.

- This approach can take advantage of Azure Cosmos DB's index for fast query performance.

The document in Listing 7-15 shows how the dates are serialized.

Listing 7-15. JSON Document with a Date Property Serialized as a String

```
{
    "id": "497c1321-0d58-4fdc-a99b-85eca0815a95",
    "firstName": "Jose",
    "lastName": "Guay",
    "birthDate": "1974-04-07T00:00:00",
    "address1": "123 Main St.",
    "address2": null,
    "city": "Chicago",
    "state": "IL",
    "postalCode": 60601,
    "phoneNumber": "3126130813",
    "_rid": "hQlzAP7VMgAKAAAAAAAAAA==",
    "_self":
    "dbs/hQlzAA==/colls/hQlzAP7VMgA=/docs/hQlzAP7VMg
        AKAAAAAAAAAA==/",
```

```
    "_etag": "\"00005d48-0000-0000-0000-59f7fde60000\"",
    "_attachments": "attachments/",
    "_ts": 1509424614
}
```

As you can see in Listing 7-15, the birthDate property is in ISO 8601 format; however, the internal timestamp property (_ts) is serialized as a Unix timestamp, which is a number representing the number of elapsed seconds since January 1, 1970. This format is available for your dates as well by implementing the UnixDateTimeConverter class. More information on the class can be found at http://bit.ly/UnixDateTimeConverter.

The two date formats have both advantages and disadvantages. The advantage of the Unix format is that it has no ambiguity. It is a clear number (of seconds) that can be easily converted into a different format. The big disadvantage is that it is really not human readable. Unless it is converted, the number has no actual meaning when read by a person. This is the big advantage of the ISO 8601 format: it can be read very easily.

An important consideration when querying documents involving date ranges is that, for efficiency and performance, the indexing policy should be configured for range indexing on strings. I covered indexing in Chapter 5.

Backing Up and Restoring Azure Cosmos DB Databases

Backing up databases is one of the most important tasks for any database administrator. Backups can help recover deleted or corrupted data from a database and can even help restore an entire database if it is accidentally (or deliberately) deleted.

In Azure Cosmos DB, data is globally distributed (or replicated) to multiple regions to provide a high level of redundancy in the event of region failures. In addition to global distribution, Azure performs full, automatic backups on all Azure Cosmos DB databases approximately every four hours. On top of this, data and backups are geo-replicated to make them even more resilient to failures.

Backups are performed in the background without affecting the performance or availability of the databases, and most importantly, this processing does not count towards your provisioned RUs.

Backup Retention Policy

A very important consideration of these automatic backups is its retention policy. Azure only keeps the last two backups, which gives you approximately eight hours to respond to a data loss issue before the data becomes unrecoverable. This is because after data is deleted, the databases are still being backed up and after eight hours there would be two backups that would not contain the deleted data.

In the event of a database deletion, the last two backups made are kept for up to 30 days. This gives you plenty of time to decide if you want to recover the database or not.

If your internal backup retention policy is different, you have to make a copy of your databases using the Azure Cosmos DB Data Migration Tool based on the schedule you need. Just take into consideration that the processing of these backups will count towards your provisioned RUs.

Restoring Databases

In the event you need to restore a database from the automatic backups, you will need to contact Azure support either by filing a support ticket or by phone. If the restore is from your own backups, then all you need to do is copy back the information using the Azure Cosmos DB Data Migration Tool.

Summary

In this chapter you learned how to create stored procedures, triggers, and user-defined functions using both methods: the Azure portal and programmatically. You saw how they work, their properties, advantages, and usages. You reviewed the concept of transactions and how they apply to Azure Cosmos DB. You worked with a stored procedure that replaced the typical call to the SDK to create documents; you also added a trigger that manipulated the document prior to insertion and you created a user-defined function that was later used in a query to report on stored data.

In the last part of the chapter you reviewed the date data type and how it is handled by Azure Cosmos DB in JSON documents. You also learned about full automatic backups performed by Azure and that to restore a database from a backup you need to file a support ticket or call Azure support.

Index

A

B

C

D

© José Rolando Guay Paz 2018
J. R. Guay Paz, *Microsoft Azure Cosmos DB Revealed*,
https://doi.org/10.1007/978-1-4842-3351-1

Get the eBook for only $5!

Why limit yourself?

With most of our titles available in both PDF and ePUB format, you can access your content wherever and however you wish—on your PC, phone, tablet, or reader.

Since you've purchased this print book, we are happy to offer you the eBook for just $5.

To learn more, go to http://www.apress.com/companion or contact support@apress.com.

Apress®

All Apress eBooks are subject to copyright. All rights are reserved by the Publisher, whether the whole or part of the material is concerned, specifically the rights of translation, reprinting, reuse of illustrations, recitation, broadcasting, reproduction on microfilms or in any other physical way, and transmission or information storage and retrieval, electronic adaptation, computer software, or by similar or dissimilar methodology now known or hereafter developed. Exempted from this legal reservation are brief excerpts in connection with reviews or scholarly analysis or material supplied specifically for the purpose of being entered and executed on a computer system, for exclusive use by the purchaser of the work. Duplication of this publication or parts thereof is permitted only under the provisions of the Copyright Law of the Publisher's location, in its current version, and permission for use must always be obtained from Springer. Permissions for use may be obtained through RightsLink at the Copyright Clearance Center. Violations are liable to prosecution under the respective Copyright Law.

Printed in the United States
By Bookmasters

Printed in the United States
By Bookmasters